APR 0 7 201

P9-CKU-594

Recipes

for a

Beautiful Life

A MEMOIR IN STORIES

REBECCA BARRY

SIMON & SCHUSTER

New York   London   Toronto   Sydney   New Delhi

Simon & Schuster
1230 Avenue of the Americas
New York, NY 10020

Certain names have been changed, some individuals are composites, and some events have been reordered and/or compressed.

First Simon & Schuster hardcover edition April 2015

SIMON & SCHUSTER and colophon are registered trademarks of Simon & Schuster, Inc.

Portions of this book were previously published on the author's blog and in *Parents* magazine.

For information about special discounts for bulk purchases, please contact Simon & Schuster Special Sales at 1-866-506-1949 or business@simonandschuster.com.

The Simon & Schuster Speakers Bureau can bring authors to your live event. For more information or to book an event, contact the Simon & Schuster Speakers Bureau at 1-866-248-3049 or visit our website at www.simonspeakers.com.

Interior design by Joy O'Meara

Manufactured in the United States of America

10 9 8 7 6 5 4 3 2 1

Library of Congress Cataloging-in-Publication Data
Barry, Rebecca, 1968–
    Recipes for a beautiful life : a memoir / Rebecca Barry. — First Simon & Schuster hardcover edition.
        pages cm
    1. Barry, Rebecca, 1968– 2. Barry, Rebecca, 1968– Family. 3. Barry, Rebecca, 1968– Homes and haunts—New York (State) 4. Country life—New York (State) 5. Women authors, American—Biography. 6. Creative ability. 7. Women—Psychology. 8. Mothers—Psychology. I. Title.
    PS3602.A77758Z46 2015
    818'.603—dc23
    [B]   2014016718

ISBN 978-1-4165-9336-2
ISBN 978-1-4165-9805-3 (ebook)

This book is dedicated to my family.
Thank you.
I love you so much.
I love you like crazy.

Contents

✱

PART THREE: Down the Rabbit Hole

PART FOUR: Crawling Out of the Rubble

Introduction

How to Get a Life

————————————————————————————

Some time ago, a few years into our marriage, my husband, Tommy, and I began to think about creating a life we really wanted to live. I was in graduate school in Ohio, about a year away from my degree, and Tommy was working part-time in New York as a copy editor for *People* magazine. ("It's a modern marriage," my mother-in-law said. "I saw it on Oprah.") Every month or so, we'd find ourselves sitting at the kitchen table with a cocktail, playing Scrabble, and having one of three conversations.

Conversation One was why my husband thought we should have a baby. He is Catholic and wanted four children (he has three siblings) and at thirty-seven years old felt it was time to get going. I'm a Quaker, was concerned about overpopulation, and was feeling pregnant enough with a collection of short stories. I was worried that once I had babies, my writing days would be over, so I kept bargaining for a few more years.

Conversation Two was how much I hated it when he beat me at Scrabble. That one often ended badly.

Conversation Three was about where we would live once I finished my MFA and what our new life would look like.

Because our jobs had a certain amount of flexibility, we weren't tethered to any particular place except maybe the East Coast, so we started with what we wanted in a town. We wanted a place where natural beauty was a big part of the landscape. We wanted to be able to live inexpensively so we could have time to enjoy ourselves and our children. We wanted to be able to walk to most of the things we needed—friends, a good coffee shop, groceries, a nice restaurant. I wanted to write fiction. Tommy wanted to fix up an old house and ultimately start a green living magazine. This was Plan A.

We thought about moving back to Manhattan, where we'd met and both lived before we got married. We knew we could get work there: Tommy had spent most of his career working at national magazines, and before I started writing fiction I had spent years writing for magazines too, often giving readers tidy solutions to complicated problems—how to quit your job, how to make gossip work for you, how to deal with the other woman who wants to steal your boyfriend (actually I never finished that one). We thought about Cape Cod, because we both loved the sea. We thought about upstate New York, where I grew up, because the area was so beautiful and will probably always be in my bones.

We decided to make a list.

"Okay," I said. "So we want someplace beautiful but not too expensive. A place where we can make a living doing what we love but not have to work so hard that we can't enjoy our lives."

"Yes," Tommy said. "Urban or rural—nothing in between. And family nearby to help with child care."

"Right," I said. "And preferably a beautiful old house with lots of character that we can fix up, and an excellent coffee shop within walking distance."

"Right," said Tommy. "Just make it close enough to the city so I can go to New York if I need to."

I wrote that down.

"And also fresh, organic food," I said. "And a house with sunporches so I can paint murals and do crafts."

"Great," said Tommy.

"And children who play quietly at my feet while I write my novel," I said.

Tommy looked at his letter tiles, then at the Scrabble board.

"That seems simple enough," I said.

"Mm-hm," said Tommy, looking at my list, which looked a little like something the princess in "The Princess and the Pea" might have come up with.

Then he beat me at Scrabble and I told him that was it—we were never having sex again, so he could forget about a baby.

Six months later I was pregnant.

I don't know how to explain this except to say that my husband just seems to have that effect on me. When we first met I was thirty-one and dating lots of people. "I'm seeing a lot of people," I said on our second date. "I don't want anything serious."

"Okay," he said.

Then I broke up with everyone I was seeing and asked him to marry me.

All I can say is that my heart knew what it wanted, and that was that.

We ended up looking for houses in upstate New York, in a small town about half an hour from the house I grew up in, where my parents still lived. It had everything we wanted—a small bistro, a bar with live music, a bookstore, and a coffee shop with great espresso. One mile east there was woodland, pastures of sheep and cows, and fields of wheat and soy. A little bit farther was the lake—deep, blue, and wide and forty miles long. Tommy was a little worried about being far away from his industry and not getting any visitors. Don't be silly, I said. (a) We'll be in the middle of wine country and all our friends love wine. (b) We won't need to make money because everything will be so cheap. "Nouveau poor is the new nouveau riche!" I said.

Tommy wasn't entirely convinced, but he loved me and knew I would be happy here and figured he could be content anywhere near water. He also knew that the lifestyle he wanted to explore if he did start his own magazine was flourishing in the area, so it was a good fit for what he wanted to do.

The first house we looked at was a brick building painted yellow, with an elegant entryway and spacious bedrooms upstairs. It was affordable, although it needed a lot of work.

"What do you think?" I said to Tommy.

"I like it," he said, and went down to inspect the basement.

I stood in the living room, looking at the vinyl folding wall that separated it from the dining room. I could still sense whiffs of the last person who lived there—the beveled mirror hanging on a wall with no sideboard beneath it, a calendar from 1972, the smell of antiseptic. I knew from the Realtor (who was my older sister, Maria, who had moved back to the area from Washington, D.C., about a year before we did and was currently looking for a husband) that the woman who owned it had died recently. The house still had that bittersweet feel of a person leaving this realm—dark carpets, dusty walls. Dim lights.

"Old woman," I whispered. "Old woman, are you still here?"

There was silence.

Then the dead woman's phone rang.

I jumped and the baby—who I was sure was a girl, I'd always assumed I'd have girls—did a backflip.

"Answer it," said Maria.

"*You* answer it," I said. "It's a ghost."

"It's not a ghost and it isn't for you, so neither of you answer it," said my husband.

But I didn't want the house after that.

"Maybe we're pushing things," I said as we drove back to my parents' house. "Maybe the timing is off and we should just go back to Columbus and wait until I graduate."

"What about that one?" said my husband, pointing to a brick building on Main Street with a For Sale sign in front.

"Oh, that place," said my sister. "It's been on the market for a while. I think the financing fell through on the last offer because there weren't any comps. It's a great building."

We made an appointment to see it the next day.

The house—a big, square, brick Italianate built in 1865—was a duplex that had been broken up into six units. It was a fabulous building: plaster walls, big windows, some still holding bubbled glass from the nineteenth century, with deep sills because the exterior walls were three bricks thick. Each apartment had its own special details: tin ceilings in one, wainscoting in another, built-ins in some of the kitchens, ornately decorated old fireplaces (five in all). Like the other building we'd seen, or maybe all old houses in the world, it needed work. There were water stains on the ceilings in several apartments, the floors slanted toward the middle of the house where the foundation had sunk after a flood, and there were bricks loose on the back wall. But the ceilings were high and majestic. And there were three sunporches.

"As is," the brochure stated firmly.

"Look!" we said. "Pocket doors!"

Tommy went outside to inspect the yard, and I stood in the downstairs parlor on the north side, which was flooded with bright light. From the living room I could see through to the mullioned kitchen window to the backyard, which sloped down through a wooded hill to a wide creek. "Old ghosts, are you here?" There was no answer. No flicker of lights, no ringing phone, just the crows calling to each other outside.

I looked out the window. I could feel the openness of the farmland that stretched a few blocks beyond Main Street.

"What do you think, baby?" I said to the baby.

It didn't kick or flutter, as if to say, "You're on your own on this one. I'm gestating."

Tommy poked his head in the door and asked me to come and see the yard. Outside, the air smelled sweet, and I could hear the creek tumbling along in the valley behind me. I looked up at the house, at the three glassed-in porches I could already imagine as candidates for a studio or writing room. I could almost feel the history of the place just by standing near it. I could feel something else too, a pulse, a beckoning that came from not just the building but somewhere deep within the land and the trees and the water that sang in the background.

If we did a few repairs, Tommy said, the rentals from the apartments could pay for the mortgage. We could live on half a New York salary and not have to work eighty-hour weeks and I could sell my short stories and write a novel while raising our kids and Tommy could start his magazine. We could get a farm share. I could ride my bike everywhere. My sister could move into the building. It could all work out. It could be fantastic.

"What do you think?" I said to Tommy when he came up from investigating one of the outbuildings. The wind had tousled his hair and he looked happy. "Should we make an offer?"

"I think we should," he said.

From the walnut tree by the old outhouse, a murder of crows rose in a shimmering black body of flight.

We closed on the house seven months later, soon after I finished graduate school. A few months later we moved in: me, my husband, our two cats, my sister Maria, and our baby, who, as fate would have it, was not a girl after all, but a boy named Liam.

Over the next two years we worked on implementing Plan A. We moved in and out of three apartments in our own building, fixing them up as we went. (Luckily Liam would sleep only in a baby swing, so his nursery was fairly easy to move around those first few months.) We bought a share from a CSA farm up the road, a green four or five acres with vegetable patches and swaths of sunflowers, zinnias, cornflower blue bachelor's buttons. That meant that once a week I could bike to the farm to pick up a supply of freshly picked veggies, and anytime I wanted I could drop by and pick flowers and seasonal herbs and berries.

We got to know the owners of the farm, Paul and Evangeline, who were in their early thirties and robust and good-humored, even though Evangeline was pregnant or nursing and farming the first three or four years I knew her. We made friends with Isabel and John, who owned an antiques store in the next town over. My older sister met and married a local winemaker named Dave and the two of them moved into an adjoining apartment. Liam turned one and began to walk—actually he began to run, which he'd been trying to do from the time he was born. I began reworking the novel in stories I'd finished in graduate school so my agent could send it out.

Then I got pregnant again.

"*What?*" I said to my husband. "How?" I mean I knew *how*. "But *when?*"

"I think it was that night you said we didn't have to worry . . . ," Tommy said.

I put my head in my hands and started to cry.

"Can't, just once, this be a happy occasion?" Tommy said, taking my hands in his.

"Yes," I said, and went to the bathroom to throw up.

Forty weeks later, three weeks after his due date, Dawson was born. That year we finished up work on one side of the house and moved into the other side. My novel in stories sold three weeks after Dawson came home from the hospital, and Tommy worked a deal out with the magazine he worked for in New York that allowed him to spend just a week to ten days in New York every month instead of three weeks.

So, we were on our way. We had the town we wanted and the old house with character to fix up, Tommy had a part-time job that gave us enough of a salary to live on, and I was carving out a living writing books.

Everything was going exactly as we'd planned.

Which should have been the surest sign that things might not turn out the way we'd imagined.

PART ONE

In Pursuit *of a* Beautiful Life

October 2007–September 2008

How to Have a More Positive Outlook

✳

October 4, 2007

Yesterday morning I was very pleased to see that my horoscope is great for October. My favorite astrologer is Susan Miller because not only does she seem uncannily accurate, she writes my horoscope as if she is looking out for me, personally. She'll say things like "Dear Pisces" (and I read "Dear Rebecca"), "You may have been feeling like you've been working hard and getting small returns," and I think, As a matter of fact, I do feel like I've been working extremely hard for small returns and I'm so glad someone finally noticed! Then she'll say something like, "Don't worry. That was because there was a quinzbykz in your something house"—my words not hers—"but now things are about to change in a big way!" And then I'll think, Excellent! Maybe I'll win an award. And I'll be happy until I realize that the horoscope is for all Pisces, not just me, and since Pisces tend to be creative people, all of us are headed for a good month and not all of us can get a Pulitzer. Still, it makes me feel like I have something to look forward to, which in general is a pretty good way to live.

My husband thinks my addiction to astrology is especially funny because there was a time in my life when I edited the astrology column at one of the magazines I worked for, and half of my time was spent adding in lines like "This would be a perfect month to clean out your address book" or "Date whoever you want! The stars are all for it!"

"That doesn't mean it was bad advice or that it wasn't true," I said.

My younger sister, Emily, a therapist and yoga teacher who lives in Oregon, agrees with me. She and her husband had their charts read to figure out what would be the most fortuitous time for their wedding. ("I'm hoping they'll be told it's at six o'clock," said my father, who is a very literal person. "What if they're told to have it at three in the morning? I'm not staying up that late.") Luckily that did not happen, although the astrologer did get a little uncomfortable when she read their charts. "Are you sure you two want to get married?" she said. "Really? Okay. If you insist. Go for June." June was beautiful, and they are still married, so obviously, the point is, horoscopes work.

Anyway, this month is supposed to be great. All kinds of special days and career leaps, etc. It's perfect timing too, because I love October. I love the dip in temperature, the way you can smell apples, grapes, and turning leaves. The way the wind seems to pick up and excitement swirls through the town around Halloween.

"Things are going to be looking up around here," I said to my husband. He was in the kitchen/playroom that is upstairs near the bathroom because we are still renovating and haven't moved our kitchen downstairs. I was in the bathroom, trying to keep the boys, who were in the bath, from drinking the bathwater.

"Don't drink that!" I said. Dawson, who is nineteen months old, just laughed and took another gulp.

Dawson is one of those alarming children who just doesn't seem to care about winning adult approval. He'll knock over his brother's trains and then climb up on the naughty chair and sit there with a pout on his face he made up, wait about a minute, get down, and knock over Liam's trains again. "Dawson!" I'll say, and he'll put himself back in the naughty chair and put on his fake contrite look. It has nothing to do with making us happy or being sorry. I think he just likes to sit in the naughty chair and pretend that he feels bad about it.

I pulled Dawson out of the tub. Then I said to Liam, age three, "Do you know what's in the bathwater? Dawson's pee."

"What?" said Liam.

"Dawson pees in the water and that's why you shouldn't drink it."

"What?" said Liam. This is what he does when I say something he doesn't like. He just keeps saying "What?" until I say something different. It's not a bad tactic, actually.

"You heard me." I went into the playroom and handed my husband the baby.

"My horoscope says my career is going to explode this month," I said.

"Great," said Tommy. "Maybe you should start working on another book instead of sitting around reading your horoscope."

But who wants to work when it's so beautiful outside? When the leaves are turning and the air smells like wood smoke and apples, and people are canning tomatoes and the trees are so yellow and orange it's almost as if they can't contain their own light?

In the bathroom, I could hear water draining from the tub. "Are you ready to get out, Liam?" I said.

"I'm just letting Dawson's pee out of the tub," he said, and took another swig of bathwater.

"Fine," I said. "Fine. If you want to drink pee, that's okay with me."

"Did you just say what I thought you said?" said my husband. "To our child?"

Yes, I'm afraid I did. If you want to drink pee, that's okay with me.

So. This is going to be a great month.

I can't wait.

 ——————————————————————————

Recipe: Butternut Squash Soup

This is an adaptation of a recipe I found years ago in a Jane Brody cookbook. I've been making this for so long that I can't remember exactly how it goes, so here's what I do.

Makes 5 to 6 bowls of soup

1. Take some butternut squash, one if it's large, and two if they're medium sized, and boil it for five to ten minutes. If you need to, cut the squash in half to submerge it. (I got this tip from my mother-in-law, Helene, who came into the kitchen one day while I was nearly cutting my arm off trying to peel a raw butternut squash. "Why don't you just boil it first?" she said. It was a very good question, and while I had an answer—"Because it will lose flavor"—it didn't happen to be correct.)

2. When the squash is beginning to get soft—just soft enough to peel easily—take it out and let it cool for a few minutes. Then peel it with a knife. Cut it open and scoop out the seeds and gelatinous goop and give them to your cat Ryely, who for some reason loves to eat it. Cut what's left into chunks, about one to two inches big, or three. (It doesn't really matter because you're going to puree it all later.)

3. Put the squash aside and cut up an onion. In a big pot, sauté the onion in butter, about 4 tablespoons. (I sometimes like to use a mix of butter and olive oil, but that's only when I'm feeling like I should eat less butter, which doesn't usually last very long.) Add salt, a teaspoon or two of pepper, and one to two teaspoons or so of curry. Stir over medium-high heat until this mixture turns yellowy brown and smells delicious, about five minutes.

4. Add chicken or vegetable boullion and about a cup of water. Bring the whole mixture to a boil. Add the butternut squash and about six cups of water, just enough to cover. Bring to a boil, then simmer for about 25 minutes.

5. Puree. (I use a hand mixer now. I used to put all of this in a blender, but it makes a *mess*.) Add salt and pepper to taste. For a touch of sweetness, add a tablespoon or two of apple cider.

✳ ——————————————————— ✳

How to Get the Romance Back into Your Marriage

--- ✳

October 13, 2007

Last night we stopped by our friends Isabel and John's house on the way home from grocery shopping and ended up staying for dinner.

Isabel and John live six miles away from us in a town that's smaller than ours. We met them through Isabel's mother, who has an antiques store up the road from us. Tommy and I had gone in looking for something we could use for storage since our 1865 house has no closets, and Isabel's mother took one look at Liam and said, "You should meet my daughter. She has children about the same age as your son."

I'll confess that the first thought I had was, "I don't see that happening." I imagined that if she had kids my kids' age she would either be like me and too tired to do anything, or well-adjusted with a clean house and children who played quietly, in which case we wouldn't have anything in common. (I'm not sure why I thought those were my only choices, but that's how I felt at the time.) Still, I wanted a friend, and a few days later Tommy and I stopped by Isabel and John's antique/curio store, which was in a former blacksmith's shop on their property.

We took to each other instantly. Our babies were just a few weeks apart, and we'd all grown up in small places, lived in cities, and come back to small places to raise our families. (John, like me, grew up here although we went to different schools and didn't know each other. Isabel had spent summers in the town where we now live, but much of her childhood was spent overseas where her father did agricultural work.) At the end of the visit I asked Isabel if she wanted to go for a walk sometime, and a few days later she came over and we put our babies in the strollers and walked around our country block, which was two or three miles long. We talked and talked, slowly venturing into more and more personal territory—marriage, love, children— finding more and more things we had in common and holding less and less back until we had walked for over an hour and the babies were starting to cry. "I guess we should go inside," I said. "Our children are getting cold."

"But we'll get together again soon, right?" we said, because we could already tell that we needed each other as much as our children needed us.

Anyway, today Isabel and John had just returned from a visit to the Amish farmstand they go to on the outskirts of town. John was cutting some tomatoes, and Isabel was talking about how great the Amish were, which she does every time she comes back from their stand.

"Why don't you just marry the Amish?" I said, as she went on about the beauty of the children, and the way they obeyed their parents and all seemed to have jobs.

"Can't," John said happily, "it's against their code."

"And they had peacock chicks," Isabel went on, unfazed.

"Yes, they did," said John, filling a copper pot with couscous. "And that doesn't mean we should, too."

"All I did was mention that it might be nice to have one or two," Isabel said. "And ever since then he's been saying things like, 'That's easy for you to say. Who's going to clean the cage?' "

"First of all," said John. "Peacocks make a sound like someone is being murdered. And foxes like to eat them."

"He's just talking to himself," said Isabel, putting a yellow flowered tablecloth down on the table.

"Believe me," said John, "I would like nothing more than to have a pride of peacocks strutting around in the backyard screaming their heads off. I just know that having livestock never ends well."

We sat down to dinner, and afterwards Tommy and John sat at the table while the children played in the living room, and Isabel and I took a walk.

We walked on the back path of their property, which winds through tall grass and an abandoned orchard, then by a flowering marsh to a pond. Actually, Isabel said, John was driving her crazy. Earlier that day they had taken their children out to the community-supported farm we all belong to to pick green beans and raspberries, and one of the younger kids had started crying. He has a yell that goes straight into John's spine, so John said that was it, they had to leave. "I said okay and walked back," said Isabel. "But on the way I wanted to pick some more beans and flowers. When I got in the car John was furious. I said, 'What's wrong with you,' and he said, 'Nothing. I'm not mad. It's just that I told you we had to go and whenever I looked back all I saw was your butt in the air.' "

I started laughing.

"Can you believe he said that to me?" she said. "Wouldn't you kill your husband? I was so mad I stopped talking to him, and then he got all huffy, like 'What, is this some new kind of torture?' And I said, 'No, it's not some new kind of torture, it's called I am ignoring you, and women have been doing it to men for centuries.' "

"At least he notices when you stop talking to him," I said. "Tommy just thinks things have gotten nice and quiet."

"We've been married a lot longer," she said.

This made us both start laughing, and then we started talking about an article I'd read about getting romance back into your marriage and how they always say things like "Schedule time for sex," or "Spend more alone time together," but no one ever says, "Get someone else to do the cooking," or "Spend more time alone reading magazines." When we got back, John and Tommy were sitting by the fireplace while the kids happily dismantled the cushions on the couch in the playroom. It was a beautiful evening—bright and cool, but with enough dampness in the air that it smelled delicious and fresh, the way autumn can up here. I remembered another article I'd read about marriage, and in it the writer had said that one of the problems with the modern incarnation of marriage is that we act as if the husband and wife are supposed to fulfill all of each other's needs—for creative inspiration, intimacy, friendship—there were a bunch of other things but I can't remember what they were because my children ran off with my brain cells. But her point was that this is a ridiculous amount of pressure for just two people and that it's even hard on the institution of marriage itself. What we should be doing instead, she argued, is cultivating lots of other intergenerational relationships outside of our marriage—with friends and family, with co-workers—that can nourish the partnership itself.

On the way home the kids fell asleep in the car. The stars were out, and the leaves, still orange even in the moonlight, glowed gently like lanterns. "Do you think it's unhealthy that instead of going on date nights we'd rather go visit our friends?" I said to Tommy.

"Of course not," said Tommy, and pointed out that when we go on date nights we have the same conversations we've been having at the house only in a different setting. "At least this way we get some new perspectives."

Yes, I thought. Like you get to see your spouse through the eyes of other adults, not just your own.

"I like you," I said, putting my hand on his knee. He covered my fingers with his.

Maybe, I thought, the problem with trying to get romance back into your marriage is that we keep narrowing the idea of what romance is. Maybe it's sometimes about going on date nights or scheduling time for sex. But maybe other times all you need to do is get out of the house and see other people, and breathe the same air under a cool night sky.

How to Unleash Your Inner Superwoman

This morning I was sitting on the couch reading a story to Liam when he interrupted me, looked at my chest, and said, "Mom, do you use your boobs every day?"

I looked down at my breasts, sitting in their underwire harness. "Not as much as I used to," I said to Liam.

"Why do you have boobs?" he said, and I told him that I used them to feed him and Dawson when they were babies. "You ate *all* the time," I said.

"Do you use them to feed people now?" Liam said.

"No," I said. "And to clarify, I wasn't feeding just anyone with these."

"Do you have milk in them now?"

"I don't think so," I said.

"Let's see," said Liam.

I took a breast out and squeezed it. (I know. But motherhood is an altered state.) A tiny jet of colostrum shot out.

"Hey!" said Liam. "You have stuff in there!"

"That's right," I said. "Mommy is very powerful."

"Okay," he said. "Put it away."

Which is the conversation we've been having about female power for centuries: "Wow! Look at that! You have stuff in there! Now put it away."

It made me think of one of my favorite Anne Sexton poems, "You, Doctor Martin."

I'd been reading a lot of Anne Sexton lately, in part because short form is easier to read when you have small children, but also because I relate to her more now.

"Really?" said my sister Maria, who often disagrees with me. She is three years older than I am, with high cheekbones and our mother's pretty heart-shaped face. We love each other fiercely, but either one of us, at any time, can start a three-day fight over something as simple as who left the fan on in the bathroom. And tension we have from sisterhood alone is heightened lately because all she wants is to have a baby and I have two, and all I want is my own apartment. "I always had a hard time reading her in college," she went on. "She's so depressing."

Maybe, I said. I might have felt that way too, back in my twenties when I didn't want to think anything was wrong. But now I just feel like she's real. It's the way she writes about motherhood and marriage, fully seeing all of it, not just what's good or what's bad. "Never loving ourselves, hating even our shoes and our hats, we love each other," she writes in "The Black Art." Or my favorite, in "You, Doctor Martin," which she wrote when she was institutionalized for severe depression after having a baby: "We are magic talking to itself, noisy and alone."

I love that line so much—I keep thinking it's how motherhood often feels. We are magic talking to itself, noisy and alone. We used to be something, in our black sleeveless tops and tall shoes. Now we are standing in front of a pile of laundry, changing endless diapers, our essence dripping onto stained shirts, stuffed into hungry mouths. Now we are invisible, even in our best skirts, lost in a small boat of dishes, dried oatmeal, and a cat that needs his thyroid medicine.

And sometimes I think motherhood *is* a particular kind of madness—one that is both irrational and tender—and this is where the soul of it lies.

Why put it away? Why stifle this place, which is vulnerable but fierce, loving yet ferocious? Why put it away when I feel crazy but know that I've probably never been more sane because I'm so tired that I'm finally saying exactly what I mean? Why not just accept that this isn't about being good or bad, it's about trying to love the people you would give your own life for, even if they make you nuts—so everyone just take a few steps back or the stuffed rabbit goes right out the window.

"Once I was beautiful," Sexton writes at the end of the piece. "Now I am myself, counting this row and that row of moccasins, waiting on the silent shelf."

Once we were beautiful. Now we are ourselves.

I did, however, put my boobs away. Even if they do have power and feed people, it's not really convenient to have them hanging out all day.

"But just so you know," I said to Liam, "mommies do have a lot of stuff. All women do."

"Oh, I know!" he said. "That's why I can't *wait* to be a girl!"

How to Teach Your Children to Clean Up

⸸

November 6, 2007

I have finally figured out how to get the kids to clean up before bed—it's a fairy I invented named Gladys. Every night I found myself picking up toys, and I sort of figured maybe Liam was still too young to pick up his own toys every night. Then one day I picked him up at Montessori school and he said, "Just a minute, I have to clean up my paints," and neatly put all his paints and paintbrushes away. I went home and said to my husband, "That's it. He's cleaning up his toys every night before bed."

So I introduced a Pick Up Fairy, a sort of grouchy fairy who lives in the woods. Every night she listens to the world, and if she hears small children saying things like, "I'm not picking up my toys," she calls the parents of that child and asks if she can come over. If the mother says yes, she comes over with a big sack and takes all the toys to her house for a week.

My thinking was that if he didn't pick up the toys, I would hide them for a week and then give them back. Liam was entranced. "What does she look like?" he said. "Does she wear a dress?"

"Yes," I said. "Every day but Tuesday. On Tuesday she wears overalls."

"Is she scary?" Liam is obsessed with scary things. It's actually a compliment from him if he thinks you're scary.

"Yes," I said.

"Does she like tights?"

"She loves them."

"What color are her teeth?"

"Green."

"Oh. Maybe she doesn't have a good toothbrush."

"Probably," I said.

Miraculously, Liam began picking up his toys every night. In fact, he has become a little obsessed with the Pick Up Fairy. "Tell me a story about the Pick Up Fairy," he started saying. Liam loves stories (I'm guessing all children do), although he tends to correct the plot midway through. "No, the monster did not go away. He kept coming closer. No, he did *not* disappear. He *ate* Liam. And Mommy cried and cried and cried forever." So I started telling stories about the Pick Up Fairy, whose real name is Gladys, and how she lives next door to the Dessert Fairy, who eats up your dessert if you don't eat your vegetables, only the Dessert Fairy is invisible, so she always wins when she and the Pick Up Fairy play hide-and-seek. "That's why the Pick Up Fairy likes to take toys," I said. "So she can see where the Dessert Fairy is."

"Oh," said Liam.

"It's amazing!" I said to Isabel later. "He picks up his toys every night."

We were sitting in her kitchen, having a cup of tea.

"Brilliant," she said, and went to the cupboard for some Girl Scout cookies, rattling the cellophane as she pulled them out.

As if summoned by a whistle, her youngest daughter, Samantha, materialized from the playroom. (Sam loves sugar and can smell it a mile away.) Isabel put the cookies on the table and I started talking about Tommy working in New York City again, which I could handle a little better when it was just me and Liam, but with two children under four, it was getting pretty hard.

Samantha tried to appear invisible.

"Sam, you already had a cookie," Isabel said.

"Take last night," I said. "Dawson woke up at four a.m. and didn't go back to sleep until six, which was when Liam woke up, and an hour later I was awakened by Maria, who was standing over my bed saying, "Get up. Both of your children have been in my apartment for the last forty-five minutes."

Isabel laughed. "At least it's your sister and not a neighbor down the street." She got up to heat some water for our tea, and out of the corner of my eye I could see Sam begin dragging a chair as quietly as she could across the room to get into the cupboard where the rest of the cookies were.

"Sam," Isabel said. "Get down from there."

Sam ignored her.

"Samantha!" Isabel said. "If you don't get down, the Chocolate Fairy is going to come and . . . chop off your hands!"

Sam leapt off the chair and ran back to the playroom.

"Wow," I said. "That's a tough fairy. Mine just takes toys."

"Yes," said Isabel. "More wine?"

"Just a bit," I said. "Wouldn't want the Hangover Fairy to come after me."

How to Manage Small Children When Your Spouse Is Traveling

--- ✳

November 9, 2007

Tommy is still in NYC and this is my fifth day alone with the boys.

Tonight I heard myself say, "Oh, for heaven's sake, cats do too use their paws to pick up!" because Liam had decided he was a cat when it was time to clean up and was picking up each individual Lego with his mouth. "Use your paws, please, Kitty," I said, and he said, "Kitty wants to use his mouth to pick up, Mommy. He can't use his paws."

I came downstairs looking something like Lizzie Borden, and Maria, whose apartment adjoins mine and who had come over for dinner, said, "I hope you have a drink tonight. You really need one. You should have several."

"It doesn't help," I said. "They're still there when I wake up in the morning. Dawson! Get your head *out* of the toilet." (Dawson, it seems, likes three things: the toilet, his brother's potty, and the plunger.)

Tommy comes back tomorrow, which is a good thing because the door to the washing machine got jammed yesterday, and I think we have a squirrel infestation in the attic.

How to Simplify Your Workload

✳

November 20, 2007

Lately all Liam wants to hear about is fairies. Yesterday in the car I told him some more about the Dessert Fairy, and how one time she came home with a whole bag of chocolates and didn't want to share with the Pick Up Fairy, and the Pick Up Fairy got so mad she threw a bag of toys up to the moon.

"No, she didn't," said Liam.

"She didn't?" I said.

"No," Liam said. "She doesn't like chocolate."

"Maybe you should tell the story," I said.

"And she doesn't get mad," he said.

"Yes, she does," I said. "That's why she comes and takes other children's toys. She used to be a very messy little girl herself, and the Good Witch, who watches over all the fairies, took away all her toys and told her she'd only be able to play with toys by taking other children's."

"What?" Tommy said. He is back from New York and was driving.

"You heard me," I said. You can't send the right message every minute.

"Well, well, well," Liam said. "You are a very messy mommy and no one takes *your* toys."

"Tractor!" said Dawson, which I think loosely translated means "Checkmate!"

"People take my toys all the time," I said. "Why do you think I don't have a swimming pool?"

"So that's where it is," said my husband. "Is that also what happened to your Pulitzer?"

"Ha, ha," I said. "Funny."

"I know what the Dessert Fairy looks like," Liam said. "Even if she's invisible, I can see her with my special eye. She has black hair, blue eyes, blue teeth, pointy green ears, and she wears a long, beautiful dress with little pink trains on it."

Then he put his blanket over his head to help him fall asleep.

I looked back at my son, covered up with a blanket like a parrot, then looked out the window. We were driving, on our way out to my parents' house, and I can't exactly explain why this happened, but suddenly I was filled with the realization that I was happy. There it was, ordinary and sweet. I turned to my husband and was about to say something about it, but Dawson started yelling himself to sleep in the back. (He's just starting to say words, but most of what he says is unintelligible, which I think is just as well. The other day he was yelling, "Ixbpcml bleepmlem mixbygy. *Mixbygy*! *Mixbygy*!!!" and I think if I knew what he was saying I'd be pretty insulted.) Then Liam pulled his blanket off his head and said, "I'll tell you a story: One day Mommy woke up. And she was biting the kitty. And that wasn't very nice. The end."

He put his blanket back over his head, and Dawson stopped insulting us and nodded off. Things quieted down and I turned to my husband.

"I'm happy," I said.

"Me, too," he said.

We settled in to the quiet of the car and my body relaxed into the seat, the way it does when the kids fall asleep and we have a blessed moment of peace and quiet, and everyone is warm and together. We drove by a snow-covered field turning blue in the dying light, and I could see the moon, pale white and blue, hovering over the horizon.

I thought of a conversation I'd had recently with my friend Denise about crises. Denise said that the thing about sadness is that it doesn't confuse you. It's there and it's hard to ignore it. Happiness, however, seems like something we have to work to train our minds to do, so when it's there, it deserves our full attention. ("I don't know," I said. "I think people are pretty adept at ignoring their sadness, too.") I think what it really means isn't that we shouldn't not feel the sadness when it comes, or work too hard at being happy—but more that when happiness does appear, just settle into that moment completely. It made me think of something that happened last summer. A friend had come to my house for dinner and had said something I thought was rude that had hurt my feelings. Later I was thinking, what are my options? I could stop speaking to that friend, although in a town this size that would be nearly impossible. I could accept his criticism and let it all go, but that seemed too hard.

So I did a meditation on it a yoga teacher taught me once, where you just ask yourself what you're meant to learn from this situation and sit quietly with it. When I did, all I saw was an image from a walk I'd been on late last summer. I was on one of the back roads by a farm when a goldfinch had come down off a telephone wire and followed me. It shadowed me for about a mile, that bright yellow against the backdrop of a field of baby sweet corn. Why, I thought later, have I been spending the day thinking about my hurt feelings instead of the miracle of a gold bird against a field of deep green, following me for nearly a mile?

Anyway, that's how we spent the rest of that car ride home: giving our happiness our full attention, settling into the moment completely.

How to Stop Worrying So Much

※

November 22, 2007

It is Thanksgiving and we spent the day out at my parents' house—my parents, me, Tommy and the boys, my sister Maria and her husband, Dave, and my other sister, Emily, and her husband, Peter, who had flown in from Oregon the night before.

My parents live across the lake from us in the house I grew up in, a Greek Revival farmhouse built in 1845 that is set back from the road up a small hill. The yard is full of lilacs and apple and cherry trees and next to the house stands an enormous poplar tree, at least five feet in diameter. I love that tree. It must be a hundred feet tall and people have often told my father to cut it down, but it's like a guardian of the house, and none of us could bear to see it killed.

When we got there, Maria was opening a bottle of wine Dave had made. Peter was playing the guitar and Emily was doing yoga in the living room. Emily and Peter always show up with vials of tinctures and yoga mats and give us yoga classes and acupuncture treatments. "We need to strengthen your heart protector," Peter said the last time he was sticking needles in me. "You have irritated wife syndrome," he said another time.

"Is that really a condition?" I said.

"How can it not be?" he said.

We were all in festive moods, as we always are when everyone is home. Mom was in the kitchen, her face rosy from steam from boiling potatoes, and Dad was putting wood in the woodstove, his black cat Goblin balanced on his shoulders. Dad worked as an administrator at Cornell, helping to find funding for community development and child abuse prevention. But he's always seemed happiest when he's chasing and photographing steam engines (his real passion), outside cutting wood, inside reading with or talking to my mother. Animals love him—it's not unusual to see him walking up to the barn pushing a wheelbarrow full of wood he just chopped, followed by a cat or a dog or a bird.

I sat down at the kitchen table and started picking at the relish plate.

"Becky!" Mom said. "That is for later. I put a cheese platter in the living room for you."

"There's too much yoga going on in there," I said, eating an olive. My mother swatted the air near my hand with her spoon.

Maria was talking about a book she was reading and then somehow we got on the subject of babies and how she and Dave were starting to try. We all thought that was good news, and then I said something to Liam about not climbing on his grandfather's desk and he ignored me.

"Do you think he's going deaf?" I said. I was worried because last week the doctor noticed a slight hearing problem in one ear and suggested we see a specialist. All I could think of at three a.m. was a time when he was six months old and Tommy was working in New York and Maria and I took him to a bar to hear a swing band from San Francisco.

(At first the bouncer wouldn't let us in.

"Why not?" I said.

"You have a baby," he said. "I can't let a baby in here."

Then he got the owner who said, "What's up?" and I said, "I have a baby," and he said, "I can see that," and I said, "The bouncer won't let me in," and he said, "Just don't leave it in the bathroom or on the pool table.")

I stuffed Liam's ears with toilet paper and we didn't stay long, but now I was worried that I ruined his life.

"But what if I permanently damaged Liam's hearing that night?" I said now. Dawson, who was nursing, patted my boob affectionately as if it was a dear old friend.

"So what if you did?" said Mom. She was wearing a purple dress and cutting celery with soft, strong hands. Mom was a psychiatric nurse by profession but she is also a wonderful cook—a skill she got from her mother, who ran a restaurant and a high school cafeteria in the '40s and early '50s. "We all damage our children," she went on. "Would you love them less? Would they love you less? You worry too much." My mother is not a worrier. My father is: he worries about the state of the world and whether he'll get things done on time or if the house will catch on fire. But my mother has this natural aura of calm that just blocks all that out. My brother-in-law Peter thinks it's because she laughs so much. I agree, but I also think it's because she's surrounded by worriers who take care of all the worrying for her.

"I think Rebecca worries too much, too," said my husband, and I thought, not for the first time, that I've somehow managed to marry my mother and not my father.

It's true, though, I do worry a lot. I worry about the plight of the honeybees and flame retardant on my children's clothes and sheets and what's in their food. I remember when I was pregnant with Dawson saying to Emily that having a baby is so terrifying in some ways, and she said, "Oh, I know—you see how little they are." But it's more like you see how little *you* are. Because you not only have to protect your child but your own heart, which has been flayed by this new love for this little thing that wants to eat all the time, and you know that if anything happens to that child, your life would be broken in a way you never knew was possible before you gave birth.

Still, the last thing a worrier wants to hear is not to worry, which I brought up later when Emily and Peter came over to see the house and how the renovations were going. (Nowhere, really.)

We'd basically given up on the house that ends up in the *New York Times* Style section after we realized that (a) we hate calling people we don't know, which makes it hard to find contractors, (b) we don't have the money, (c) we have two small children.

We started talking about the different ways people communicate and how much trouble it causes, and I said, "For example, maybe I do worry too much, but I think there's a nicer way to say it than, 'You worry too much,' which is dismissive."

I think Tommy said something reasonable like we just see things differently. He thinks the kids eat fabulously and are healthy as horses and I keep worrying that they are going to get sick.

"When I look at your kids I see two emotionally and spiritually robust little people brimming with life and humor," said Peter.

"See?" I said. "Now I'm not worried," I said to Tommy.

"That's because someone other than me said it," he said.

"You're handsome," I said.

He went up to bed and Emily went off to watch TV and Peter and I stayed up drinking.

"Here's the way I see it," he said. "You're a mother. How could you not be worried?" He went on to explain that in Chinese medicine worry is associated with the earth element, which is the sympathetic element that takes care of everything. "Like one, giant, worried mother," he went on.

"That's right," I said. "And who wants an unworried mother? Someone who is detached and peaceful—someone you can never get a rise out of. Where's the fun in that?"

"Exactly," said Peter. "Sometimes I worry my wife is getting dangerously close to enlightenment, and then she'll be so blissed out who will take care of me?"

"Ha ha!" I said. "Cheers!"

Later, though, I was thinking that all the worried person wants is for someone to tell them it's going to be all right. To listen to their concern and say, "It's okay." It's okay—your rage, your worry, your love, your sadness. It's all okay.

Then I thought about how much time I spend telling my children it's okay. Or it's not okay. It's okay to be sad. It's not okay to wrap the cat in the down comforter. It's okay to be mad. It's not okay to throw your sippy cup at your grandfather.

I wonder if God/the gods/the Universe feels the same way about us, watching us run around banging our heads against the walls, complaining about what we don't have, ignoring what we have. We must seem like such infants, and maybe God (who I think is a woman) is just kind of sitting up there like a giant mother saying, "It's okay." It's okay to feel mad. It's okay to feel sad. It's okay. You're okay. I still love you, even if you do chew up half the life/world I made for you. Now please, please, just try not to drive so fast. Is it too much to ask you not to ruin the ocean/Amazon rainforest/kill all the whales with your seismic testing? Why can't you just share? If you can't play nicely, I'm taking it all away.

Don't make me come down there.

I mean it.

 ——————————————————————————

Recipe: Worried Mother Cure

Ingredients:
1 mother with one or more children
A few self-help books
A friend who has taken a meditation class

Sift through.

Try these:

1. Give yourself a certain number of minutes of the day to worry. Set a timer. Worry like hell, and then stop. (I got this tip from a behavioral psychologist I interviewed once. It did not work for me but might for you.)

2. Repeat your worry out loud two hundred times. Be sure to do the full two hundred. By the time you say "I am afraid I've ruined my son's hearing by taking him to a bar and stuffing his ears with toilet paper" two hundred times, it seems a little smaller. (Same psychologist: this did work.)

3. Bring yourself into the present moment. For example, when you're up in the middle of the night worrying, just say to yourself, "Right now, I am safe. The kids are nearby, everyone I love is okay. My children are safe. My husband is alive. My body is warm, my head is on the pillow. Right now, in this moment, I am fine." I got this from a life coach/minister who also said, "And you know what, honey? If the worst thing happens, you'll manage."

4. My friend Elvina says her meditation teacher told her that when she is up in the middle of the night worrying, she is to interrupt her worries with a list of delights she'd experienced that day, instead of listing all the horrors.

5. If none of this works, I like to think about Wangari Maathai, who helped people to plant over 30 million trees in Africa, and Gandhi. Neither of them seemed to spend too much time worrying. They just got up in the morning and did what they needed to do to change the world.

 ———————————————————————

How to Get the Help You Need

✱

November 30, 2007

How do single parents manage? They are *superheroes*.

Tommy is gone again and yesterday Liam got an ear infection and now he can't sleep. His ears hurt, he has a fever. Nothing makes him feel better—ibuprofen, Tylenol, nothing. He's been unable to put his head down for more than fifteen minutes without waking up in pain.

I haven't slept in two days, I can't keep him from crying. Then today I got into a huge fight with Maria about leaving the heat on, and she said that ever since I became a mother I'm much more high-strung. Then I said something about it being harder than she thinks, which was probably a mean thing to say given how much she wants a baby, and she slammed the door between our two apartments. Liam started crying, and then Tommy called and I burst into tears and told him his job was killing me and he had to come home, because all I do is yell at everyone.

"I only have a day left," he said.

"I know," I said. "You just can't be gone all the time anymore." In the background I could hear adults talking to other adults in mature, calm voices. No one was screaming. No one was refusing to take a bath. They were all talking quietly and getting things done.

In the reflection in the window of our kitchen, my hair looked like Medusa's.

"Do you want me to come home tonight?" Tommy said.

"No," I lied. "I'm fine." Why can't I handle this? I thought. It's just two children. It's just an earache.

He was quiet.

"Well," I said. "I'll see you tomorrow night."

Tonight I got the boys to sleep at eight, but I was too wired to fall sleep until eleven and Liam woke up at one thirty. I brought him into bed with me so I wouldn't have to keep getting up, but every time we'd both fall asleep he'd wake up and start crying again. Finally, at five a.m., I didn't know what else to do so I put Dawson on the couch in Maria's apartment and got into the car with Liam. He sat in the back, nodding off and then crying as I drove around on empty moonlit streets, so tired, near tears myself, saying, "Shh, honey, oh Liam, I know it hurts. We're going to the doctor later today. I'm so sorry. Please, please stop crying," and thinking, I cannot do this one more second, I can't, I can't, I can't. I need Tommy. I need sleep. I need a shower.

Finally, *finally*, Liam closed his eyes and his breathing deepened. I drove a few miles just to make sure he was really down, and then pulled into our driveway, where I gently turned off the ignition. I lay my head on the steering wheel and sat there, wondering why no one told me it would be this hard, and if they did, why I didn't listen to them. Sometimes I think this is the most difficult thing about being a mother—you're almost never alone, and yet there are these days when you feel so lonely.

After a while the car began to get cold, so I picked Liam up carefully and carried him back into the house, praying that I could rest for an hour or so before Dawson got up. As soon as the door shut, though, he woke up again and started crying.

It was 5:37 a.m. I hadn't slept in two days.

I think I was on the floor in fetal position when I heard the stairs creak in my sister's apartment. Her door opened and she came into the dining room where Liam and I were both crying. She didn't say anything, just gently unbuckled Liam and picked him up from his car seat, and motioned for me to go upstairs.

My whole body melted. Thank you, I mouthed, but her back was already turned. I went upstairs and fell down across my bed with all my clothes on including my shoes, my whole body like lead. In the apartment next door I could hear my sister walking back and forth, talking to my son in a soft, sweet voice. "It's *okay*," she was saying. "It's *all right*, little baby." I'm so sorry I was a jerk earlier, I thought. I'm so sorry. You were right. I am more high-strung since I became a mother. It's because sometimes I feel like I'm drowning.

Next door I could hear Liam's crying slow to a hiccup, and eventually, I, too, drifted off to the sound of my sister's rhythmic footsteps on the old pine floorboards, the lilting beat of her words. "It's all *right*. It's *okay*, little baby. Don't cry. Everything is going to be fine."

How to Quit Your Job

✳

December 2, 2007

Tommy came back from a week in New York yesterday, and today when we were in the car coming back from getting groceries, he said that his company was offering a severance package for people who volunteered to be laid off, and he was thinking about taking it.

"The union isn't as strong as it used to be," he said. "And this is probably the best package I'll get."

"Do you *want* to volunteer to be laid off?" I said.

"I'd get to keep my salary and health benefits for six months," he said. "And then unemployment benefits."

"And you wouldn't have to travel anymore."

"Right," he said. "And I could work on my magazine proposal."

I looked out the window, turning the idea of Tommy quitting over in my mind. On the one hand, it would be so great to have him home all the time. On the other hand, both he and I were aware of how much work magazines are—we'd both worked at start-ups where toiling till three in the morning wasn't unusual. And what about health insurance? And money? Tommy's job in New York was perfect for our life here. We could live on his part-time salary, and while I hated how much he was gone, it was only a week here and there (although somehow it always felt longer).

Still, I'd never seen him so happy professionally as when he was a managing editor, which he was when I met him. And this idea for his own magazine hadn't left him. In fact, lately it was crystallizing. "It's like all the things people say are impossible to do or too hard or too expensive—solar energy, organic food, straw-bale houses—are actually happening here," he said the other night. "All we'd have to do is show what they're doing." We were at a farmers' ball at the Grange Hall. All around us were young farmers in their twenties and thirties, some with children. Everyone seemed happy and alive—the men with their sunburnt faces, the women with their hair in braids or ponytails, wearing bright dresses and earrings with burgundy tights and muck boots.

"I know," I said. "You could do a fashion story with the people in this room alone."

Then the band started playing and we took our children upstairs to dance.

"Do you really want to start your own magazine?" I said now.

"I think I do," he said.

"They're pretty time consuming," I said.

"I know." He paused. "I like being a copy editor, and I'm good at it, but I know there's more I can do with my life."

I thought about losing benefits. I thought about how when I decided to leave freelance writing for women's magazines to write a collection of short stories, he said, "Of course you should do it," knowing full well it would cut our income in half.

"I think you should do it," I said.

"You do?" he said.

"Yes," I said. "It's your dream." We can always live on less money or work more, I thought. None of that is as damaging as saying no to an idea that's taken root in your soul.

"Okay, then," he said.

We drove the next few miles in silence. I felt a rush of panic mingled with a weightlessness, the exhilaration that comes with the type of decision that looks bad on paper but that somehow at the same time feels completely right.

Later that night we worked out a plan. If he took the next six months to work on the proposal, we could live on his severance. I would help him with the editorial vision and also finish my novel proposal. Then, if the novel sold, we could live on that while he tried to get financing for his magazine.

"But then what?" I said. "Will we have to move back to New York?"

I didn't want to go back to New York. I loved our town—how we'd found Isabel and John, and how we moved back and forth between each other's houses, sharing gossip and childcare. I didn't want to be far away from my sister or parents. I loved seeing the same people every morning at the coffee shop down the street, the fresh flowers, the way we'd effortlessly gotten our kids into the Montessori school that was only eight miles away and had goats, a turtle, and a rabbit the size of a beagle named Mr. Babbins.

"Maybe not," he said. "A lot of what we want to cover is already happening here, and it would be great for overhead if we had the offices in a small place."

"And we could create jobs," I said.

"That's what I was thinking," he said.

And wouldn't it be great to live where we worked? To actually have an exciting job in an office in an old building down the street? To not have to telecommute, which is lonely, or even a regular commute, which means driving? To create our own publication where we could write whatever we wanted, and work with whomever we wanted?

"How much do you need?" I said.

"Four and a half million dollars," he said.

"I have a quarter," I said. "But tomorrow we can buy a lottery ticket on the way to drop the kids off at school."

• • •

So, Plan B: Tommy quits working in New York and is home full-time to work on a business plan. I finish my novel proposal and get an advance that we can live off while Tommy finds funding for his magazine. Genius! I don't know why we didn't think of it earlier.

How to Get Along with Your In-Laws

*

New Year's Day, 2008

We are in Ohio visiting my husband's parents, and today my mother-in-law, Helene, and I were in the kitchen, looking at the cookie plate my sister-in-law Kim had made—chocolate drops decorated with red and green M&Ms, frosted cake lollipops, and some kind of brownies with mocha icing. "She is so good at presentation," I said. "These look amazing."

"I know," said my mother-in-law. "I'm lucky if I get my cookies out of the oven, let alone on a plate."

"At least you make them," I said, happy to see her.

Helene is nothing if not real. Her kitchen has piles of papers all over it, and at the top of one is an article about how piles of papers indicate a psychological difficulty with letting things go. This line is circled and underneath it she's written, "We have a psychological problem!"

This morning my mother-in-law came down in her nightgown. "I'm going to wear this all day," she said, sitting down. "Rebecca, your hair looks like a helmet."

"Ha ha ha ha ha ha," said Liam and Tommy.

"Did you sleep on your face?" said my mother-in-law.

"You know," I said. "In some families it isn't considered proper to attack someone else's hairdo first thing in the morning."

"That's the only way I can see that your hair would get like that. My hair looks like that in the back in the morning. It goes every which way. But that's because I sleep on my back."

The real reason my hair looks this way is because I am traveling with small children. Liam won't go to sleep without Tommy lying down with him and Dawson keeps bashing into things. I keep saying that it's because the children are out of their routine and the house isn't baby-proofed, but I think the truth is more like we're all out of our routines and none of us is baby-proofed.

The good news is that my horoscope says this will be an excellent year. Lots of travel opportunities and a project that is near and dear to my heart is coming to fruition.

So here are my New Year's resolutions:

1. Try not to take everything personally.
2. Learn to be up-front with people I love in a productive way instead of bottling things up and holding grudges. (So far this has meant saying, "When you say 'Rebecca is a saint' after spending a few hours with my kids, is that a compliment?")
3. Something else, I forget what—probably "be more organized" or "finish my book proposal."
4. Stop eating sugar for three weeks. (Maybe two, depending on withdrawal.)
5. Be more consistent with the children. My sister-in-law says it worked wonders on her dog. (Although her dog, much like my children, never stops jumping.)
6. Assume more goodwill on the part of others. (It turns out that "Rebecca is a saint" actually *is* a compliment.)
7. Once a day, say out loud five things I'm grateful for. Coffee, for one. A warm house, for another. My family. All of them, includ-

ing Tommy's mom who made enough chocolate chip bars to last for a month.

8. Help Tommy with his magazine.

9. Lose the last ten pounds of baby weight.

Meanwhile, last night Dawson actually ate five plastic grapes off a hat rather than the meal I put in front of him. Which is only slightly better than last week, when I tried to feed him an egg and he lay down on the floor and started crying, then took a bite out of my deodorant.

"The real question," said my agent, after she asked if my child was still alive, "is why you have a hat with plastic grapes on it."

"It was my Easter bonnet six years ago," I said.

"Only from you would that make sense," she said.

How to Lose Your Baby Weight

✳

January 15, 2008

This morning in the car Liam said happily, "Mommy, you're fat."

"Liam!" I said. "That is not a nice thing to say." I was trying to drive, which I actively dislike doing.

"But you *are*," said Liam. "Your belly is fat because I was in there."

"That's true," I said, "it was very big when you were in there. But what makes you think I'm fat now?"

"Daddy said so," Liam said.

"*What?*" I said, nearly hitting a cyclist.

"And you said so," Liam said.

"Oh," I said. I did say something to my sister Maria the other day about wanting to lose a few pounds. (Ten, to be specific.) And then I remembered my doula telling me before I went into the hospital with Liam, "When you leave the hospital, you'll look like you did at about five months." What she didn't say is that you look like that for the rest of your life.

"So what?" I said now. "Mommy just has a nice round tummy."

"It's fat."

"Liam," I said. "Ladies don't like to hear that."

There was a pause. "Do daddies?"

"Ha, ha," I said. "Yes, they love to hear it. All daddies love to be told they're fat. Every day."

"What about aunts?"

"I wouldn't try it," I said.

"Are you a bad driver?"

We pulled into the driveway to my mother's house, where we were spending the afternoon. I opened the back door to the kitchen and was greeted by my parents' black dog, Stanley, who is old and graying and a lot like my father, who has a gray beard and dark hair and even now at nearly seventy has a lightness to his step, as if he can't wait to get to where he's going next.

My mother had a towel draped over her shoulders and was cutting the stems off green beans. Dad was out by the barn, stacking wood.

"It's warm in here," I said.

"I turned on the heat," she said. "Don't tell your father."

"Grandmama!" Liam said. "You have the biggest bottom in the world!"

"Hi, sweetie," said my mother.

I sat down and told her about the comment Liam had made in the car. "It's too bad he thinks that's a negative thing," she said.

"I know," I said. "I'm not entirely sure that he does. But at the same time, I don't know if he should be running around telling people they're fat."

"He can say it to me," said my mother. "I would just say, 'That's right. I'm nice and big and soft.' " I laughed. My mother *is* big and soft. She wasn't always—when she married my father she was about the same size as me (8–10) but then she had children and they moved to the country. Dad was traveling a lot and she started putting on weight, and by the time I was eight or nine she was pretty heavy. It never seemed to bother her that much. Once when I was in second or third grade I came home from school upset because I'd overheard someone say a teacher I loved was ugly.

"You know, some people might say I'm ugly," Mom said matter-of-factly.

"What?" I said. I couldn't believe that was true.

"Sure," she said. "I'm fat and I have thin hair." She said it not as if it bothered her but just as a fact of the world, and I remember looking at her and thinking, How could anyone say that about you? You're so beautiful. She still is. She has a serene brow, and kind, intelligent eyes, and a pretty face lined with good humor. She radiates calm, warmth, and quiet strength.

Later, as I got older, my feelings about her weight became more complicated. I admired her strong sense of self, but I worried about the way she took care of other people at the expense of her own health. I would read statistics about overweight people being at risk for chronic disease and heart failure. I was afraid of losing her and wanted to protect her, so I would go home and try to get her to eat differently or try water aerobics. Once, sick of being harangued by me, she said, "I think those magazines you work for have really warped the way you see things. If I was thin and smoked cigarettes, this wouldn't bother you."

I said this wasn't about how she looked, it was about me not wanting her to die.

"Everyone dies, honey," she said calmly, which was true but very dissatisfying when you're trying to tell someone you love them.

Now she's in her early seventies, and she didn't die. And sometimes I wonder if some of why I spent all that time worrying had to do with wanting attention. My whole life my mother has been busy taking care of people—running a support group for people who were trying not to hit their kids, housing women who had just left their husbands and had no place to go, protesting the Vietnam War, becoming a psych nurse, driving women who don't have cars to and from jail to see their loved ones, teaching nonviolence in maximum security prisons, etc. I love this about my mother. I love that this is her life's work, that she has an ability to see the light and the darkness in people, and to see what's funny and true about them at the same time. I love the way she can talk to anyone, the quiet, surefooted way she can raise the level of any political conversation by reporting what she's seen.

There's a specific loneliness that goes along with being the child of a saint, though. You love them, you admire them, but there's a part of you that feels like, What about me? I have problems too. And then you feel embarrassed—of being jealous or needy. So you say, "I just want you to take care of yourself," which makes them say, "Oh, for heaven's sake, I'm fine," and what you're trying to say, sometimes at least, is, "I'm not."

I thought about all this as I drove home with Liam—what it means to me to be called fat, what it means to her, how I don't really like it, how she doesn't care. How much time I've spent worrying about her when I could have just been enjoying her.

It's just like my kids, who want to start asking me questions the second I'm on the phone. Maybe that's all we're doing when we worry about other people. We're just asking for love any way we know how.

Later, Liam said that he didn't think I was fat anymore.

"But you are a bad driver," he said.

Noted.

How to Silence Your Inner Critic

✳

January 18, 2008

This morning I turned in my proposal for the novel I've been working on based on a character from my first book—an oftentimes drunk advice columnist who never follows her own advice.

"So it's based on you," said my sister Maria.

"No," I said. "I follow my own advice about twenty-five percent of the time. It's *other* people who never pay any attention to it. Liam—oh my *Lord*. What is that on the back of your pajama leg!"

"Chocolate!" said Liam, twisting around to see what I was talking about. "I put it in my footies in case I get hungry in the middle of the night."

"Now see," I said to my sister, "I would not advise that."

"And yet somehow it's not a bad idea," she said.

Anyway, the proposal is done and today was unseasonably warm, so I got out the baby buggy my sister-in-law got us for Christmas and attached it to Tommy's old mountain bike. I decided I'd get some exercise and ride Dawson around our town, which has two moderately steep hills. We hadn't gone more than twenty-five yards before Dawson started shouting.

(A few words about Dawson's voice. It is loud and high-pitched, like having a very demanding peacock in the backseat. Once we went to the Sciencenter, where there is a booth that registers noise level. Dawson went into it and started yelling, and his voice rated higher than a lion's roar. "Warning," the machine said, flashing red lights and blinking. "Constant exposure to this sound could cause hearing damage.")

"*Mommy!*" Dawson yelled. "*That's Daddy's bike! Not yours!*"

"Dawsie, this is Daddy and Mommy's bike."

"*No! That's Daddy's bike! You should be very careful!*"

I turned to go up a small hill, which wasn't easy hauling a thirty-pound child. I was standing up off the seat, huffing and puffing, trying to get up the hill when finally I gave up and turned around.

"*No!*" Dawson yelled. "*Town that way!*"

"Sorry, Dawsie," I said. "We're going back home."

"*No home!*" Dawson yelled.

It must be hard for two-year-olds, I thought. They feel like they're finally getting to the point where they can tell us what they know—that avocados are intolerable as a snack food and walls are for drawing on—and we refuse to listen or we change things like bedtime on them. I completely understand. I often feel that way about work, like I've finally figured out some kind of a solid narrative arc for a story, and then a character will do something like decide to cheat on his/her spouse or go to Hawaii instead of getting sober and I feel like yelling, "*No! Plot that way!*"

"No home!" Dawson yelled again. "Town!"

"Sorry, honey," I said. "You're too heavy."

There was a brief silence.

"*Mommy* too heavy," said Dawson, a little more quickly.

What? I thought.

"No," I said carefully. "Mommy's so *pretty*."

"Mommy so *heavy*," Dawson said.

So.

That's how I spent the rest of my ride—biking a baby buggy up Main Street with a two-year-old in the back shouting, "Mommy so tired. Mommy so *heavy!*" and me shouting back, "No! Mommy's so *pretty!*"

"I think I'll just keep this baby weight for a while," I said later to my sister and Isabel when I had put the baby buggy in the shed and the boy down for a nap. "Anyway," I went on, "I tried dieting for a few days last week, and I gained three pounds."

"You know what that means," Maria said. "It means you shouldn't diet."

"You could also just buy some new clothes that fit," said Isabel.

Those seem like much more sensible solutions.

That night I dreamt that I took the kids to New York City and left them in Brooklyn by mistake.

How to Work with Your Spouse

✱

February 1, 2008

Yesterday, Tommy and I set up our offices, and he officially created an LLC for his magazine and put me on the payroll.

"Excellent!" I said. "Can I work on my book and write my blog when I'm supposed to be working for you?"

"No," he said.

"It's what everyone else in America does," I said.

"It will be bad for the other employees."

"What other employees?" I said.

"Me," he said.

Anyway, I start work for real next week. Can't wait. Then I can have an affair with my boss. My horoscope was right—things are definitely looking up around here. My life is about to take a scandalous new turn.

Meanwhile, tonight I put little plates of organic hot dogs and peas in front of Liam and Dawson. I went to go get them cups of organic juice diluted with water. When I came back to the table, Dawson had the wand from my sister's mascara in his mouth.

How to Celebrate Your Success

                                                ✶

February 15, 2008

My agent called today to tell me my novel proposal had been accepted. I was so excited, I decided to keep the pair of very expensive boots I had bought the last time I went to New York.

"I can keep them, right?" I said to Tommy. The book sold for about half of what I'd hoped for, but enough for us to live on if I write it in a year.

"Yes," he said, adding that advances don't really mean anything, that what matters is that I write a good book and someone is offering to pay me to do it. "You should be jumping up and down, happily," he said.

We went out to dinner instead, and the next day I wore my new boots to take Dawson to day care.

"You look nice," said Dawson's teacher when I dropped him off. "Are you going to a meeting?"

"My novel proposal sold," I said.

"Congratulations!" she said.

"Thank you!" I said, and stopped myself from saying, "Also, I just really like my new shoes," because then I would sound like all the girls in the toddler room.

· · ·

Later my mom called.

"I heard the news!" she said. "Good for you! How much are they paying you?"

I told her. There was a pause.

"Is that going to be enough for you to live on?" she said.

"It is if I write it in one year," I said. Although the last book took me seven years. And now I have two children under four. Still, I just have to carve out time to work on it. Three to four hours a day. I'm convinced if you work three to four hours a day you will have at least something done in a year.

"I think they should pay you more," she said.

"Thanks, Mom," I said.

Last Sunday, this is what I heard Tommy saying to Dawson on his way out the door to church this morning: "Dawson! We're just going to church. You don't need your helmet."

That all depends, I thought. It all depends.

How to Civilize a Two-Year-Old

✳

February 20, 2008

February! There is no worse month. Every year I say I
like winter and every year I mean it until February. It's the cold. The
relentless gray. The way we're all involved in this abusive relationship
with the weather. When I lived in San Francisco and the weather was
nice for thirty days in a row, I would walk around thinking, "Oh, you
people are in so much trouble. You're going to pay for this someday,"
because here where I'm from if you get a sunny day, you pay for it
with two weeks of gray ones.

Today was blustery and too cold to go outside, and Liam and Dawson were home sick, which means they have low-grade fevers and tons
of energy. How are you supposed to continually entertain people this
small? By four o'clock we had played with blocks, built a fort, and
made some kind of attempt at arts and crafts using rocks and poster
paint. Finally, we all sat down in front of the TV, and I turned on an
old movie called *The Ghost and Mrs. Muir.*

Liam immediately started asking questions. "Is that a ghost? Is he
sad? Is he a real man?"

Dawson, meanwhile, was lurching around in the background like
a baby Godzilla, throwing blocks and pushing things off tables. Dawson is a very physical child. He has a big head in comparison to his

brother, and when he gets frustrated with Liam, he just rolls on top of him. Earlier in the month, a cupboard door from one of our kitchen cabinets fell on his head, and he just batted at his ear as if discouraging an annoying fly and kept moving toward the yogurt pops. And he loves throwing things. "Dawson," I hear myself say, "don't throw that. Don't knock that over. Leave the kitty alone. Dawson! Put the toaster down!"

("You sound the way I used to on the psych unit when there was a full moon," my mother said. "People would get so crazy by the end of the week, we'd all be hearing voices. Usually mine, saying, 'Keep your pants on. Don't set yourself on fire. Put the TV *down*.' ")

Tommy said that he had just read a new book about handling toddlers. The theory behind it was that we go through all the evolutionary stages of humankind in the first years of our lives and that basically toddlers are little Neanderthals.

"So you have to treat them that way," my husband went on to explain. For example, when they say, "I want cookie," and you say, "You have to have dinner first," they think, "You big dumb thing! I said *cookie*! Not *dinner*," and start screaming and throwing things because they can't make themselves understood. So what you have to do is say, "I know you want a cookie. But we have to have dinner first."

We were in the car on the way home from the food co-op.

"*Bottle!*" Dawson started yelling. "*Bottle! Bottle!*"

"I know you want a bottle, Dawsie," I said gently, trying out what I'd just learned. "I heard you. But we don't have a bottle in the car, so you have to wait until we get home."

Dawson got quiet. Then he lobbed a sippy cup at my head. "Soccer ball!" he said happily.

Then this morning I was in the living room watching Liam play with trains. I had fixed myself a plate of eggs and was sitting in a rocking chair balancing them on my lap when Dawson lumbered in, pushing a table with all his might across the floor. He had a very stern look on his face. "No, Mommy!" he said, shoving the piece of furniture ahead of him like an ant pushing a piece of gravel. I thought he was going to use it to climb the bookcase and knock all the books off the shelves, but he pushed the table up alongside my chair, then took my plate away from me and put it on the tabletop. "There!" he said firmly.

I mean really. Who died and made him the Martha Stewart of baby Neanderthals?

"Tommy!" I yelled up the stairs to my husband. "Get down here! Dawson's evolving!"

Dawson handed me a fork.

"All right, fine," I said. "No more eating in the living room without a table. But you need to start pooping in the toilet."

"Zombie!" Dawson said, and went into the kitchen to discover fire.

How to Tame Spring Fever

--- ✳

March 15, 2008

Well. It is impossible to get work done right now. Everyone has spring fever. According to the paper today, one of the local landlords entered one of his tenants' apartment, punched him in the face, yelled obscenities, and threw a small television into the sink. According to the gossip I heard at the coffee shop, he also threw a futon down the stairs, and the tenant, who was also his best friend, had to climb out of the apartment in his pajamas and run up the street barefoot to a bar to call the police.

"Those two have always had a complicated relationship," one of the regulars at the coffee shop said. "They used to be roommates and once one of them went to Vermont for the weekend and packed the remote in his suitcase, just to drive the other one nuts."

"It's the weather," I said.

It's the middle of March, and when I woke up this morning there was snow on the ground. *Snow!*

I almost went back to bed. Everyone has been going crazy. Dawson was up for four hours in the middle of the night a couple days ago, and Tommy and I had a fight on Sunday about how long it takes to do the dishes.

("Don't feel bad," Isabel said. "John and I had a fight the other day because he wasn't leaving the house fast enough."

"I was making a sandwich!" John said.)

Yesterday I heard myself tell Liam that if he kept riding his Big Wheel around the living room, I was going to throw it in the Dumpster. He started crying huge, terrible tears, his whole chest heaving, begging me not to do that to his bike.

I said fine, fine, I wouldn't put it in the Dumpster, but he absolutely couldn't ride that thing in the house.

He wiped his eyes and said, "Oh, thank you, Mommy."

Then, in a more normal voice, "What is a Dumpster?"

I told him it was a scaly monster with horrible yellow teeth that loved Big Wheels.

Meanwhile, this was the conversation we had last night at Maxie's, where we went for dinner because school was closed due to an ice storm and we needed to get out of the house. "Mom," Liam said. "Can you tell me a story about Ryely"—our black cat—"and the zombies?"

"Maybe after dinner," I said.

"Do zombies eat people?" he said.

"Yes," I said.

"Do we have zombies in our basement?"

"No. There are no zombies in New York State. Zombies only live in Florida."

"I really hate zombies," Liam said.

"Liam," Tommy said, "*hate* is a very strong word. In this family we try to say 'I don't like' or 'I don't care for.' "

Although "I really don't care for the way the oil companies treat the environment" doesn't have quite the same ring to it as "I hate those greedy bastards."

"Do you hate children?" Liam said.

"Of course not," I said. "I love children. Especially you and Dawson."

"Well, I don't care for zombies," Liam said, and picked up a crayon and began to color.

Outside, we heard the lonely whistle of a freight train. *"Whoo! Whooo!"* shrieked Dawson, causing a woman at the table next to us to drop her knife.

"Inside voice, Dawsie," said my husband.

"This is my inside voice!" yelled Dawson.

"Oh look, a train!" I said to Liam. "Can you see it?"

"I see it!" Liam said. "There's two diesel engines! And one more! And a hopper car. Hopper car, hopper car, hopper car. Tank car!"

Liam, like my father, loves trains, and there is a story my grandmother used to tell of my father doing the exact same thing when he was about Liam's age, watching a freight train pull into a station in Pennsylvania. I sat listening to his recitation, letting the wine warm my blood, feeling nostalgic and happy that my son responds so enthusiastically to something his grandfather so dearly loves. I turned to Liam to give him a kiss and caught him just as he was about to jab the waiter in the butt with a fork.

"Liam!" I said. "For God's sake! Don't do that!"

"I just really hate coloring," said Liam.

Fortunately the weather report for next week is sunny with temperatures above freezing, which should be good for everyone, especially the crocuses, who keep trying to bloom in spite of themselves.

Hours spent working on novel this morning: 3 (would have been 4 if I hadn't been home writing up all the gossip I heard at the coffee shop)

How to Get the Job You Want

--- ✳

March 18, 2008

Yesterday was Dawson's second birthday, which was so sweet. He was so excited—about having people in the house, about the prospect of a cake—that he started saying happy birthday to everyone he saw. "Happy birthday!" he said to our tenant Pam, the midwife and artist who rents the upstairs apartment. "Happy birthday!" he said to Mark, who manages the coffee shop and is remarkably tall and blond and looks like a displaced Viking. ("It really depends on the year," Mark said.)

Then when we had the actual party and the cake came out and we sang "Happy Birthday" and he realized that the party was for *him*, Dawson almost fell off his chair in delight.

"Happy birthday *Dawson*!" he said. "Oh! Happy birthday *me*! *I* happy birthday!"

They just enjoy *everything*, these little people. Sometimes I look at them and think, How do you do that? How do you walk around with such an open heart all the time? It's amazing.

Meanwhile, Tommy and I have been trying to put together a column for me to write for his magazine. I have given him some samples of pieces I'd written about the kids, but he keeps saying they don't have enough of a news hook.

"I hate news hooks," I said. Largely because they mean I have to do research that doesn't involve talking to people I know.

I showed him a column in one of our local papers that I really enjoy. In this particular piece the narrator had knocked the cell phone out of the hand of someone who had answered it in a movie theater while the movie was playing.

"See?" I said. "He just tells a little vignette. No grand, sweeping conclusion, just a funny, slice-of-life story. That's what I want to do."

"But he touches on something universal," my husband said. "Everyone hates people who talk on cell phones during movies."

"Everyone thinks things that little kids say are funny," I said.

He looked unconvinced.

"You look unconvinced."

"Do you want to read about raising children?"

"Not if you say it like that," I said.

"I just think people like to read about things besides kids," he said.

"I'm not just writing about kids," I said. "I'm writing about family and community and what it's like to try to build a life for ourselves."

"I'm not saying you can't write about that," he said. "I'm just saying you have to tweak things so they apply more to current events."

"That would mean I would have to start reading the newspaper," I said. "Which makes it harder for me to sleep, which makes me a horrible mother."

I went into the playroom to check on the kids and found that a big patch of wallpaper had been torn off the wall, leaving a chunk of exposed plaster. (Not to be confused with the chunk of plaster that's actually missing from the wall along the stairs. "How much would it cost to fix that?" I asked the last painter/handyman who came through a week ago to deal with an uneven ceiling. "I really don't care to do that kind of work," he said. "You mean you won't?" I said. "I don't *care* to," he said. "Once plaster starts falling . . ." Then he just sort of shook his head and shuddered. We decided it would be easier to hang a picture over it.)

"What happened here?" I said, looking at the wall.

"We wanted it to look more haunted!" said Liam happily.

More?

"I'm going to the gym," I said.

"Oooh, can I come?" said Liam. "Are you going to ride the bike that goes nowhere?"

"Yes," I said. "That is exactly what I am going to do."

Possibly for the rest of my life.

When I came home I told Tommy I wasn't going to write for him anymore. That lasted about ten minutes.

The good news is I'm almost done with chapter one of the novel. Linda Hartley has almost left New York. Experiment seems to be working.

How to Be the Life of the Party

--- ✳

Easter, 2008

According to my horoscope this past weekend was supposed to be a great one for romance. Well. Ha. Ha ha ha ha ha ha ha. If Easter is all about rebirth, I died and came back a shrew. I'm just not getting enough sleep.

Last night Dawson woke me up at three a.m. going through his happy birthday wishes like he was saying a rosary. Then he sang a little John Denver song he learned at school to himself, and then he said, "Mommy seeping. Daddy seeping. Liam seeping. Dawson *awake!*"

I lay in bed, too tired to get up, hoping he'd go back to sleep, which was when he started yelling, "Mommy! Mommy! Mommy-mommymommy! *Get up! Get up, Mommy!*"

Then came the tears, so loud that I thought he'd wake up Pam in the apartment next door.

I dragged myself out of bed and went over to soothe him.

"Tooth *huuuurt*," he said sadly.

"Oh, honey, why didn't you say so?" I said, rubbing his back and giving him a little Motrin.

"Oh," he said gratefully. "Happy *birthday*, Mommy."

I went back to bed but then Liam started coughing, and then I was up and couldn't get back to sleep until five.

I am so, so tired. I might actually be going crazy from it.

So this morning was Easter Sunday, and I snapped at my husband because I didn't think he was getting up with the kids in the morning enough, and he said I needed to get better about asking for help, and I said, "You don't respect me," and he said, "That's not true," and I said, "I know!" and jammed a bonnet on my head and we all went to our friend Michael's house for an Easter parade.

Michael is a sculptor who lives in a restored farmhouse near us— a white clapboard building surrounded by fruit trees and a sculpture garden, with a pond and a garden lush with lilacs. The house was full of Michael's friends—farmers and cooks and gardeners and bartenders, and a few teenagers skulking around looking for places to make out. On the table was a rack of lamb, fondant cupcakes, a giant salad, and a plate full of grapes, oranges, and dates.

I set Liam and Dawson up at a card table with some toys and told Isabel, who was there with John and her children, how little sleep I was getting. She said she had just read an article about some new studies that said that sleep deprivation, like hard narcotics, actually changes the way the brain works, which I completely believe. After a week with no sleep, I'm so short-tempered and impatient and weepy I don't even recognize myself.

In this condition, I went on, it is not easy to write about a single woman looking for a husband and having a great time drinking at a bar. I keep writing these asides for my main character, like, "What she did not know is that years later she would look back at this time and think, 'At least I could sleep in until seven thirty in the morning, noon if I was hungover, and didn't have half-sized little people climbing all over me saying, Mommy, come look, Mommy, *get up!* Mommy, can you please wipe my bottom, Mommy, look at this bead I pulled out of my nose with my own two fingers."

"Why is it," I said, "that the one time in your life when everything really needs consistency—your children, your novel, your house—is the same time that you keep getting curveballs like teething and the croup and a flooded basement, which make consistency impossible?"

"I don't know," she said. "David, don't step on the eggs. I think the answer is just to give in to the chaos. The people who can do that are the ones who get out alive. Or less scathed anyway."

"Oh fuck," said Liam, who had been trying to erase a pattern he'd made on an Etch A Sketch egg.

"What?" I said.

"Fuck," said Liam earnestly. "This stupid thing is broken."

"Liam," I said, trying not to laugh. "That's not a nice word."

"I didn't say it to a person," he said. "I just said it to this dumb, broken thing."

"If it makes you feel any better," said Isabel, "this morning I stepped on the new rug I bought for the kids' room and someone had peed on it, and I still don't know if it was the dog or Sam."

"That does make me feel a lot better," I said. "Thank you."

"No problem," she said. "What are friends for?"

I sent Liam outside to find his father, and when Tommy brought him back in he was crying as if the world was ending because Tommy wouldn't let him strip naked and jump into the fountain.

It was all enough of a distraction that Tommy and I were friends again by the time we got home, and everyone went to bed early. And then this morning both our children woke up so happy to see us, their faces so bright at the sight of ours I fell completely in love with them all over again. It reminded me of something Tommy said he'd gotten from a book he's been reading about money. In it the author said that most people have already started complaining before their feet even hit the floor in the morning, which is not good for future success. But my children wake up so happy and excited about the new day, and that's an amazing and wonderful thing to be around. When do we lose that? (Seventh grade, I think.) More important, how do we keep it?

"You are the light of my heart," I said to Liam when I came out of the shower. Liam smiled as if that was old news, as if it was something he'd known forever, and pointed to a fantastic structure he'd made out of blocks.

"It's a cat city," he said. "The whole planet is orange."

Hours of writing accomplished today: 3, in spite of many
    conspiracies against me, not the least being that I sprained two
    fingers on my left hand in yoga attempting to do a headstand
    away from the wall

How to Manage Sleep Deprivation

                                                       ✳

March 31, 2008

More sleep deprivation! Last night Dawson woke up at 2:30 a.m. I checked his diaper (dry), hushed him, and rubbed his back (useless). Then I gave him a little homeopathic remedy in case he was teething, which made him so happy he climbed out of bed to play with his toys.

"Sorry, baby," I said, putting him firmly back in his crib. "You'll have to cry it out."

He cried from 3:10 to 5:16.

For those of you like me who have difficulty with math, that's *two hours and six minutes.*

Then, when he finally stopped, Liam woke up. "Mommy!" he said. "There's something scary in my room!"

"It's your brother," I said. "Go back to sleep."

But then Liam had to be soothed, and I didn't get to sleep until 6:00 a.m.

At 7:30 the little monsters woke up. Dawson was up first, yelling three of the twenty-five words he knows.

"Mommy! Get up! Get up, Mommy!"

Tommy got Dawson out of his crib and put him in bed with us, and then Liam came in and they both started climbing all over me saying, "Get up, Mommy! Get up!"

"What is it with you two?" I said, even as I pulled them close to me. "Mommy Mommy Mommy! Why don't you ever bother your father?"

"We just want to love you all the time, Mom," Liam said matter-of-factly. "That's all. We just want to love you every minute."

My poor rattled, sleep-deprived heart sprang open. I pulled them onto my lap. It's like living with starlight, these boys.

Of course I forgave them everything.

Well, almost everything. I think I used to have a better complexion.

Recipe: Soothing Mommy Face Mask

This recipe was inspired by my friend Rachel, who has studied plant medicine and makes her own skin-care products. One day when I asked her what to do for my skin, she said, "Do you have an avocado at home? Okay. Mash it up, smear it on your face. If you want, you can add a banana."

Here is my recipe:

1 tablespoon mashed fresh avocado

1 tablespoon plain yogurt

½ teaspoon honey

Some jojoba or almond oil (I've also used olive oil. "So you're almost
    wearing a salad," Tommy said to me that time. "Ha ha, very funny," I
    said. At least it's not a roast chicken.)

A drop or two of vanilla extract or essential oil if you want this to smell
    good

Put all of the ingredients in a small bowl or cup. Mix them to-gether with a wire whisk until the consistency is creamy. Apply gently to your face. Keep on for 15 minutes. Rinse, and follow with a moisturizer, if you'd like.

Of course, the other possibility is that my skin is simply getting older and there's nothing I can really do about it. But whatever. Sometimes it just feels good to put some food on your face and lie down.

 ————————————————————

How to Be a Dilettante

✳

April 5, 2008

Yesterday I put the little statue of Ganesh my mother brought back from a trip she took with my sister to an ashram in India up on my desk. ("Mom isn't paying attention to any of the rules," my sister wrote to me in the middle of the retreat. "She keeps talking. Her dorm is the loudest one."

"You can't put twenty women in a room and not expect them to talk," my mother said later. "That's ridiculous. I don't care what kind of God you're into.")

Anyway, Mom said Ganesh is known as "The Remover of Obstacles," and is also a patron saint of arts and letters. "He can make your journey go much more smoothly," she said, and since I'm working on a novel and Tommy's trying to start a magazine, two things we've never done before, I thought now would be a good time to start making him some offerings.

"Good idea," said Emily, adding that I should put him on a red cloth. "And he likes sweets."

I put a little pile of jelly beans in front of the statue. Yesterday, Liam discovered it.

"What's wrong with that elephant?" he said.

"That's Ganesh," I said. "He's a Hindu god, and we have to be very nice to him."

"He has arms," Liam said, eyeing the jelly beans.

"You can't eat his candy," I said.

"But he doesn't eat it."

"I know, but it's an offering, and if we take it back he might not like it. Like if someone took away your Easter candy."

"Like you stole all of my Easter candy out of the eggs?"

"That's different," I said. "I'm just keeping it safe for you."

"That's just a statue," Liam continued. "It can't eat anything."

"It's symbolic," I said. "Why don't we go look Ganesh up and find out more about him?"

"I don't want to," Liam said. "I want to eat the jelly beans."

"You can't eat Ganesh's candy." I felt a battle of wills coming on.

"I don't like Ganesh!" Liam said.

"No, no!" I said. "We love Ganesh! Your father and I do not need any more obstacles."

I finally gave him the candy.

"I want the jelly beans!" Liam said. "Can't we just give Ganesh stickers?!"

That night at Isabel and John's, John's mother said that Ganesh is a jolly, fun god who would probably like stickers. In fact, she added, he'd probably be willing to share his candy. That's a very nice quality in a god if you ask me.

Anyway, now it's almost nine, and Dawson is in his crib yelling, "Lie down and be quiet!" at his father. Only, because of Dawson's pronunciation (he is much more interested in full sentences than carefully saying each word—which was kind of how I spoke French when I was living in Paris and, I now realize, doesn't fool anyone), it sounds like "LIE dowblaehade KIET!" Tommy has just firmly shut their bedroom door.

Oh well. At least Dawson very clearly says, "Mommy is so pretty." (It only took three months for me to train him.)

Hours spent writing today: 2.5, with interruption by my friend Rebecca, who is in for the week from Italy. It's too gorgeous outside, really, to think too much about a novel.

How to Get Your Children to Go to Bed, Part 1

———————————————————————— ✳

April 13, 2008

Yesterday we piled into the car and went over to Isabel and John's for tea, which turned into dinner. When we got there, Isabel, wearing a new sundress she got at a tag sale, was putting a round of Camembert on the table.

"I've been so self-indulgent lately," she said, opening a bottle of wine. "I've decided we're getting older, and being skinny won't make us prettier."

I thought this was such a pleasant observation I ate most of the cheese.

We started talking about a parenting book from the seventies she'd been reading about how to talk to your children. The book suggested remembering that children have reasons for everything they do, so we should try to understand and address them. Which is the same thing my mother has always said: Everyone has a perfectly good reason in their own mind for whatever they're doing, no matter how crazy it seems. Even if it's wearing a football helmet to cross the street, or offering a policeman a cocktail when you've gotten drunk and stolen his car.

"For example," she said. "Last night David (her four-year-old) was trying to take apart a pen, but it was bedtime and he didn't want to go to bed, so he started getting upset and yelling, 'I don't like you.' "

She decided to follow the advice from the book and knelt down to his level and said, "You seem mad," and he said yes, yes he was mad. He wanted to play with his pen and did not want to go to bed. "I said, 'I can understand how that must feel, that's no fun,' " Isabel said. " 'But now it's bedtime.' " (That's another trick in the book—not to apologize or say "Do you want to go to bed?" but just say "It's bedtime, period.")

" 'So let's put this away and you can play with it tomorrow,' " she added. And he said okay and went to bed.

"He said okay," I said, "and went to bed? Just like that? Amazing. I need to use that on Liam."

Liam hates going to bed. Hates it. Dawson goes down like a lump, but Liam gets up, leaves his room, comes out to see what Tommy and I are doing, or to tell us that his kitty (the stuffed animal he sleeps with) has a sore throat, or that he (Liam) accidentally broke his foot and needs some juice.

That night, true to form, after I read him two stories Liam threw himself across my lap and said he wasn't going to bed, he was going to lie right there all night and never go to sleep again.

"It's bedtime," I said firmly. "You have to go to bed."

"No!" Liam said. "I'm just going to lie here on your lap."

"You can't, sweetie," I said. "I have to get up and do things."

"But I hate going to sleep!" he said. "I just hate it!"

"Liam," I said. "What is so horrible about going to sleep?" And he said, "Waiting for sleep is so lonely!"

Well, I thought. You've just explained my twenties.

I got up and gave him a book. "Look," I said. "Take this book and look at the pictures, and you can imagine that all the people you like in this book are in your room keeping you company. That's what mommy does."

"Can I have a monster book?" he said.

"Let's try Olivia or Frances instead," I said.

He was asleep in ten minutes. Genius!

Then I went into the office, where Tommy and I got into a tense discussion about work. I feel like we're living in a house of stagnation: The roof still leaks. We can't figure out how to make the upstairs fully usable. I'm not getting my work done because I'm not getting enough sleep.

"And what about your business plan?" I said. "Is it close to being done?"

Tommy sighed and said it was still going to be awhile. He had been taking an online course on how to write a business plan and had expected to have his done by the end of this month. But one of the things he'd learned in the class was that the scope of his project was complicated and required a lot more research. Other things kept coming up, too, like applying for health insurance for the kids, or finishing up last year's taxes, or a tenant's furnace or sink that needs to be replumbed.

Isn't that always the way it goes when we're going after a big goal? I thought. We set our sights on them, but then they seem so scary and/or risky that we turn to something safe, like doing taxes. I completely understand it, but I wonder how many people's dreams have been extinguished that way. It must be the number one saboteur—the safe, boring thing.

"And I don't want to ask you for help," he said, "because you have so much to do."

"I know," I sighed.

I slumped down on the couch, next to the piles of papers I'm sorting through for my book, which are next to the piles of papers he's looking at for his magazine. Across from me by the window was a bag of clothes we need to take to the Salvation Army and a fax machine we rarely use, a half-eaten chocolate bar, and our cat Ryely, staring at us with large green eyes, as if to say, "Clean this shit up."

"I think it's just hard that both of us are taking risks at the same time," Tommy said.

"I know," I said.

How were we so naïve when we made our original plans? What kind of time did I think I'd have once I had children? But I didn't know. I didn't know how I would want to be with them all the time and yet want to be alone, how they would wake me up at night and get coughs and viruses and earaches. I didn't think those things would take up so much space. I didn't know how invisible I'd feel to the rest of the outside world, which is busily moving on without me. I didn't know how hard it would be to write and how hard it would be not to write. My children know when my mind is someplace else. They know when I'm living in another world, and they do everything they can to pull me out of it. I didn't know how hard it would be for my husband, who loves to be around groups of people and, now that I think of it, has always worked in an office and almost never worked at home, to start a business by himself.

"Maybe we should Feng Shui our office," I said.

Although I suspected that our problem is deeper than whether or not my desk faces the window.

Hours spent on the novel this week: 25

Hours spent trying to work on the novel this week, but spent
    sending out freelance articles and pitches to help cover the bills:
    about 8

How to Fall Back in Love with Your Life

── *

May 3, 2008

Today was such a beautiful, happy day. It was warm and sunny, and suddenly, as if it happened overnight, the trees have bright, baby green leaves on them and the redbud trees and cherry trees are all blooming. Flowers are coming up everywhere—daffodils, the lavender in our tenant Pam's garden, and tiny blue violets on the lawn.

Yesterday Isabel and John came over with their kids and I made a big pot of vegetable biryani that tasted awful (at first) because I didn't cook it long enough, so we all had some bourbon to give it time to absorb more flavor and that put us in excellent moods. Tommy and John played badminton in the backyard while the kids ran around and Isabel and I sat on the back porch, discussing an article I was writing for a women's magazine on how to get along with your family.

I looked up and saw Liam tearing down the hill on a little plastic turtle with wheels my mother-in-law bought him.

"Liam!" I said. "Slow down!"

I had been telling him all week not to ride that thing down the slope of the yard, which ends in a sharp drop-off full of pricker bushes. Since I had told him the next time he did it I would take the toy away, I bent down and took it away.

Liam was appalled. He cried and cried and told me he hated me.

I tried to be calm and adult, even though it was the first time he had ever said he hated me, and it hurt.

"Honey, I know it's hard to get a consequence," I said. "But why didn't you listen to me?"

"That turtle doesn't go very fast," he said. "And I told you I know how to stop! And you weren't supposed to take that away from me!"

"It sounds like you didn't feel like I listened to you," I said, and went on to say something about how no one likes to be ignored, and I don't like it any more than he does, and then I asked him if he was ready to say he was sorry and he said no but he threw his arms around my neck, which I decided was apology enough for the time being.

We went back to the house, where dinner was ready and everyone was busy putting their plates of food together. Liam settled in at the kids' table and dinner turned out fine. Later, after everyone had left and things settled down, a rainstorm came. I was in the kitchen washing the dishes, feeling happy and full of everything—life, good company, good food—when I looked out on the back porch and saw Liam sitting quietly on a chair eating blueberries from a cup, watching the rain fall.

Liam is almost always in motion, and for him to sit still, absorbed by the sound of the rain, was such an unusual sight I almost held my breath the way you do when you see a rare bird or wild animal that doesn't know it's being observed.

He stayed out there until I finished the dishes, and then I went out and sat down next to him. It was lovely out. The sky was that deep evening blue it turns just before it becomes night, and the trees were silhouetted against it. Across the creek I could see the lights from someone else's window and the rain poured and poured down. Is it because we're mostly made of water that it is so soothing to listen to rain fall? It's as if our bodies respond to it gratefully, like *thank you, thank you, thank you.*

I put my chin on Liam's head, smelling his gritty, little boy hair. "I'm sorry I didn't listen to you today," I said. "And I'm sorry I yelled."

Liam just nodded.

"Do you think we can try to listen to each other a little better?" I said. "Then we won't have to fight as much."

Liam shook his head. "No," he said gravely. "We'll always be fighting." He said this as if it was a bit of heavy knowledge he's had for a long time. "People will always be taking things away from other people."

We were quiet.

"Well," I finally said, "the good news is that people will probably always be giving things to other people too."

Liam didn't say anything.

"I'm pretty happy now, though," I said. "Are you?"

"Yes," he said, and then added, "it's because we aren't bumblebees. They just hate the rain."

Hours spent writing this week: a nice, solid 30

 ————————————————————————

Recipe: Vegetable Biryani

This is a great dish to throw together anytime, and you can use almost any seasonal vegetables. It was inspired by a book called *Thirty-Minute Vegetarian Recipes* by Mary Gwynn (1995), which I borrowed from my brother-in-law Dave. He uses it all the time. It's a great book for easy, healthy vegetarian meals, but it might be hard to find.

Serves 6

2 onions

2 carrots

1 parsnip

1 potato

Half a head of cauliflower (or broccoli, or mix of both)

1 tablespoon safflower oil

½ cup green beans, cut in half crosswise (That's too hard. I usually skip those and put in half a bag of frozen peas instead.)

5 to 6 tablespoons biryani paste (You can buy this at any supermarket
    with an Indian food section. There is a way to make it from scratch,
    but my friends who are chefs recommend making your life a lot easier
    and buying it in a bottle.)
1 ½ cups basmati rice
1 cup canned chopped tomatoes, undrained
3 cups vegetable stock or broth
Salt and freshly ground black pepper
Fresh cilantro and raisins for garnish

1. Chop the onions and the other vegetables. (To make this a less boring task, invite a friend over to keep you company while you work. For best results invite someone who (a) is a good storyteller, (b) is a good listener, (c) has her own kids and doesn't care if you have to wait for the food to season, or (d) all of the above.)
2. Heat the oil in a large saucepan over medium heat. Add the onion, carrot, parsnip, and potato, and cook 5 minutes, stirring occasionally until slightly browned. Stir in cauliflower, broccoli if using, and green beans (or peas). Continue cooking one minute more.
3. Stir in the biryani paste and rice and cook one minute. Add the undrained tomatoes, stock or broth, salt, and pepper. Bring to a boil, then reduce heat, cover, and cook 15 to 18 minutes, until the liquid is absorbed and the rice is tender. (I mix the raisins in here.)
4. To serve, fluff with a fork and garnish.

✳ ———————————————————————— ✳

How to Organize Your Bathroom

May 25, 2008

Spring is out in full force and the whole town is responding. The boys shoot out of bed like rockets, ready to climb things and ride bicycles the moment they're awake. In fact, the whole town seems a little excited. This morning at the coffee shop everyone was in a good mood, half of them sitting on the benches by the front windows, soaking up the sun. The sparrows are having a convention in one of the bushes at the far end of our yard. The crows are screaming too, but they're always mad about something.

After coffee, I went for a long walk outside of town, which took me past fields full of baby sweet corn, ditches full of bright-blue cornflowers, and a farm full of lambs and heifers leaping around. I was following the advice of my acupuncturist, whom I went to see because I was feeling a little light-headed. He said this was normal for spring. Everything rises, which means all the energy rises to our heads, which makes us a little crazy. He suggested I go for a nice long walk by a stream to reconnect with the earth and redirect my attention downward, to my feet.

I needed some grounding, too, because Tommy has gone to Ohio to help his parents move and I have been alone with the children for a week. In some ways it's easier with one parent, because I don't have to battle Tommy over when they should go to bed, or whether or not they should cry it out. ("The thing you really need to do," said my friend Lucy, "is to get divorced. Being a divorced parent is great. You get to make all the decisions when you're alone, and then several nights a week you can go out with your new boyfriend."

"I know!" I said. "The only trouble is I like my husband."

"That *is* a problem," she said.)

In other ways, it's a lot harder.

Tonight the boys were in the tub, and this is what I heard myself say: "Liam! Do not lick the scrub brush! That brush is disgusting!"

I couldn't remember exactly why it was disgusting, but I had a vague memory of saying recently to myself, I should throw this out, and then thinking, Oh, I might as well keep it. It's not like anyone is going to put it in their mouth.

"Am I being naughty?" Liam asked.

"No." I sighed. "I guess not. I never *told* you not to lick the scrub brush. But if you do it again, you'll be naughty."

"*My penis!*" Dawson shrieked as if he'd just discovered electricity.

I took a diaper into the other room to throw it out, and when I came back Liam was swinging on the shower curtain.

"Liam!" I said, as the shower curtain rod slowly gave way. "For heaven's sake! Oh, honey, you broke the curtain rod. Daddy is going to be really, really mad."

"*My feet!*" shouted Dawson happily.

"I guess *that* was naughty." Liam sighed. "Sorry. I just really felt like swinging."

Well, what are you going to do? Sometimes if you feel like swinging, you just have to swing. Speaking of which, it looks like frat boys live in this house. There are clothes all over the bathroom and this morning I woke and on my bedside table there was a half-empty bottle of pinot noir and a half-drunk cup of coffee from the day before. We're running low on food, and I suppose the lawn needs attention. Yesterday at the coffee shop, Kevin, one of the men I have coffee with in the morning, said, "I think I saw a lion lurking in the savanna behind your house."

I'm not even going to get into what the kitchen looks like.

How to Make Your Kitchen as Chic as Your Wardrobe (or How to Decorate an Old House)

✳

June 15, 2008

It is June, which I didn't think could be more beautiful than May, and yet it is. There's so much green everywhere right now. The wooded area that extends from our backyard down to the creek is full of sweet-smelling phlox, which Liam said yesterday looks like a purple ocean. We were playing Mama Bear and Baby Bear, which consists of us walking around the backyard to look for butterflies and new flowers. I had just said, "Well, Baby Bear, what do you smell?" and he'd said, "The sky," and I said, "What does that smell like?" And he'd said, "The wind."

Last weekend we drove to my grandmother's house to pick up some furniture, because it's clear that my grandmother, who has Alzheimer's and is now living in an assisted living facility near us, won't be going home and my aunt wants to sell the house. Among the pieces we brought home was a kitchen table with eight chairs. I had always loved that table, but I wasn't exactly sure where we were going to put it, because our kitchen is long and narrow and the table is kind of big. It settled into the room perfectly, however, almost like it was made for it. I keep feeling that way about our house in general. We paint and move things around and rearrange furniture, but the house seems to have its own ideas about what it wants and where things should go.

It's like this with repairs, too. Every time we come up with a new wall to break down or someplace to put in closets, someone will come and say, "No, no, that's a load-bearing wall," or "I wouldn't do that there, the whole ceiling could come down." In the end, what I think this place wants is to be restored and maintained, period.

In any case, I was so happy about the kitchen table, I called Isabel and told her she should drop by and see it, and she said the table was perfect and that we should christen it immediately. Then my sister brought over some bread and wine and cheese, and I said something feebly about needing to work, but Isabel said that was ridiculous and pointed out that I had had an exhausting weekend.

"Look at this," said Isabel. "It's a beautiful day and here we all are sitting around the table enjoying each other's company. *This* is living."

I cut some bread. "I do feel a little guilty," I said. "Today is the first day I've had in almost a week to write. But my tooth is killing me." (I had had a root canal retreatment a week before.)

"You've been miserable ever since that tooth started hurting," Isabel said. "What are you taking?"

"Prescription ibuprofen from my last C-section," I said.

"How many milligrams?" she said.

"Six hundred," I said. "And it expired a year ago."

"Oh, Jesus Christ," she said. "Take some medication! Here! Take four of these right now," she said, taking some ibuprofen from her purse.

"Thank goodness," said my sister. "I've been telling her all week to take more medicine."

"I still listen to Isabel because I've only known her for a few years," I said. "Don't worry, it will wear off."

I took the pain meds and we started talking about marriage, and the way the kids try to divide and conquer the second they're born.

"Only they're so little, you can't actually get as mad at them as they make you, so you turn on each other," said Isabel.

"Oh, I know," I said. That made me think of a time a few days ago, when Dawson was yelling at the top of his lungs and I was trying to put pants on Liam, and Tommy asked me where his hairbrush was, and I snapped at him.

What I'd meant was, "My brain cannot handle one more sound, one more question. I have been trying to explain to a four-year-old that he has to wear pants for the last five minutes, and that information has depressed him so much that he is now weeping and kicking me and my tooth hurts and I should be working on my novel and Dawson's voice is about to split my eardrums."

Instead I said, "I don't *know* where your hairbrush is," and only just stopped myself from saying, "Did you check up your ass?" (Which I'm pretty sure would not have been a nice thing to say.)

Maria said maybe we needed a date night, and I said maybe we needed to just accept that these years when the kids are young are hard on a marriage, and stop trying to make everything perfect. Marriage is long. Maybe you have a few tough years, so what? Maybe that's just normal. I love my husband, I know he loves me. Can't that be enough for a while?

"Except that then your husband goes to his high school reunion and has an affair with his high school sweetheart and you get a divorce," said my sister.

"What?" I said.

"I'm just saying," she said. "It happened to a friend of mine."

"There had to be other factors," I said.

"She might have had a little drug problem," said my sister.

By now it was four o'clock, and John showed up with Sam, Lucy, and David, and then Tommy went to pick up Liam and Dawson and it was dinnertime, so I suggested that everyone just stay for dinner. Then I invited our tenant Pam, who lives in the upstairs apartment on the other side of the house and who happened to be walking by while

Tommy was getting Liam and Dawson out of the car, and she came over with some beer she made.

It was a perfect lost day.

I used to have days like this much more often when I was a denizen at a local bar—you know, those days when you know you have responsibilities, but you just let pleasure take over instead. I have always thought they were important for good mental health, but I haven't had many since I became a mother. And at some point during all this, I remember looking up and thinking I should be working, but there was Dawson sitting on Isabel's lap, and Liam and Isabel's daughter Sam were helping me with the vegetables, and I thought, No, this is exactly what I should be doing. I should be here, enjoying this day and the kitchen table I inherited from my grandmother that can fit this extended family we've made from our friends and housemates.

In the middle of it, Tommy came up to me, a little drunk, and put his arms around me and said he missed me. And there it was. Open affection between us in the middle of the kitchen. Just like that.

I leaned into him, smelling his skin.

Later, I said something about the lost day to Pam after everyone else was gone and I was doing the dishes while Tommy put the boys to bed. We had been talking about her divorce, a friend of hers who is fighting breast cancer, my sister's desire for a baby, and life in general.

"I *am* worried about not getting work done, though," I said.

"Don't," she said. "You'll get it done. And you know, the older you get, the more you realize that everything else, the jobs and responsibilities and worries, they all fall away. And what you're left with is this." She spread her arms and opened her hands, gesturing toward the room, the house, the blue night outside. "Ordinary days when you were happy."

So here's to the beginning of summer and to a perfect lost day. To any day, really, when you enjoy each other without trying.

Recipe: A Lost Day Platter

1 wedge of white cheese (I like brie, but a strong sharp cheddar is also good.)

Figs—fresh if you can get them, cut in half, although dried will also do (My friend Michael says you can soak them in brandy for an hour or so before serving, then eat that with the cheese.)

1 wedge of some kind of blue cheese (We use Lively Run Drunken Goat cheese, which is made near here. It pairs nicely with the figs.)

1 loaf of fresh bread, artisanal if you can find it

1 jar of green olives (Preferably the kind that come in a nice glass jar that you might not normally buy, but since the day is all about pleasure, why not?)

1 bar of dark chocolate (Very important, especially if you have a toothache. It pairs nicely with whiskey.)

2 to 3 bottles of wine

A bottle of good bourbon if you can find it

2 to 3 pears cut up in slices

Arrange all these items on a big table. Serve at three in the afternoon on a weekday when you should be doing something else.

How to Teach a Child to Let Go

———————————————————————————— ✳

July 20, 2008

Yesterday was my grandmother's ninety-seventh birthday and we went out to my parents' house to celebrate it. (This is my grandmother with Alzheimer's, the one whose kitchen table we inherited.) She lives nearby and still tootles around on her walker, vaguely wondering who I am and why I brought these small people to her room to play with her hairbrushes. Sometimes she throws a cane or some food. Other times she has moments of pure, disarming sweetness. For example, she is pleasantly surprised daily by the fact that she has a cat. Every morning it comes out from under the bed and she says, "Oh, hello! Who are you? Where did you come from?" as if the animal is a gift from the gods (which it probably is). Or she'll look at me on a day I haven't showered because I was up at night and say, "What a beautiful dress you're wearing," and I just want to kiss her.

The last time we went to visit her we brought the kids with us, but they kept climbing on the chairs and quickly figured out how to turn the gas fireplace on and off, so Tommy took them outside. My grandmother and I sat next to each other in the drawing room, with long moments of silence between brief exchanges of conversation.

"Mom and Dad are in Mexico," I said, and she said, "Oh, that's nice," and I said, "How has your day been?" and she said, "Nice, I think. I can't remember most of it." Then I said I'd just talked to one of her daughters and she said, "I hope she's well," and I said, "Yes," and then Dawson came running in and turned on the fireplace and Tommy took him out again. "Is that one yours?" my grandmother said, and I said, "Yes."

"How do you like being a mother?" she said, and I said, "Some days I'm just so tired."

And she looked at me and smiled and said, "Yes. I know," and patted my hand.

And then she left her hand on mine for a minute and squeezed it. And I squeezed hers back and we just sat there.

Tonight, however, she didn't want to be touched. I think it might have been hard for her to be someplace other than her room, but she seemed confused—barely connecting to anyone, talking to my mother as if she were a maid. Mostly she sat there and petted Stanley, my parents' seventeen-year-old dog, who has recently taken a downturn in health and can barely lie down comfortably.

Maybe sensing this, Liam and Dawson played quietly, and at the end of the night my grandmother gave them each one of the birthday balloons we'd brought for her. On the way out to the car Liam let his go by accident. It happened before any of us could stop it: one minute it was on his wrist and the next minute it was irretrievable, floating up in the sky, higher and higher and smaller and smaller.

"There it goes," I said, trying to minimize the damage. "Off on its own adventure."

"It looks small," said Liam, and then he started to cry as if his heart would break.

"Oh, Liam," I said. "Honey, it's okay. We'll get you another one."

But Liam was inconsolable. He sobbed in the backseat, as if he was fully experiencing the difference between one moment when everything is fine and everyone is having a great time, and the next, when something we love is gone. Tommy and I tried reasoning with him, but nothing worked, and in a way I understood. When I had watched the balloon go, I had felt a tug of sadness too. Maybe it had something to do with seeing my grandmother, so small and unreachable in her old age, retreating farther and farther away from us into an interior life I can't see or understand. Or maybe it just had to do with the fact that there's nothing worse than hearing your child cry over something he loved and lost without meaning to.

"Oh, Liam," I said, "I'm so sorry."

"It's just that it's gone," he said woefully. "And I'll never get it back."

How to Plan the Perfect Family Vacation

*

August 7, 2008

In the car, at eight p.m., hour three on the way to Cape Cod for our end-of-summer break, Liam asked if we were going to our summer house. I thought that sounded a little grand, since we don't really have a summer house but have the use of a much-loved but very old little cottage that has a flower growing up through one of the floorboards in the dining room, which my father and uncle inherited from my grandparents.

"It's not our summer house. It's more like a house we get to visit sometimes in the summer."

"Yes it is, it's our summer house," said Liam.

"I can see how it would seem that way," I said, "but it's really Boppy and Uncle Davey's house."

"I want a summer house!"

"You and half of New York City," I said. "Go to sleep."

Silence. Then Liam began thrashing around and muttering in his own language he's created to keep himself from falling asleep.

"Liam," I said, "stop thrashing. It is eight o'clock and when you start acting like this, it is a sign that you are tired. Now settle down and go to sleep."

It was quiet for a moment in the backseat.

"Where's the sign?" Liam said.

"What sign?" I said.

"The sign that I'm tired."

Tommy started laughing.

"I meant that it's an indicator."

"Will you make me a sign?" he said.

Tommy laughed. "Yes. Mommy can make a sign for you that says, 'You Are Tired. Go to Sleep.' "

"That's what I want," said Liam.

"Okay," I said. "And it will probably be more effective than anything I say. Now it's quiet time. Go to sleep."

Liam and Dawson finally fell asleep and our vacation began. Which meant that Tommy and I had a fight.

It started out innocuously enough. I was talking about a book I'd read about that took a plot from a classic and modernized it, and Tommy said, "I'm telling you, that's the way you should go."

"What do you mean?" I said.

"I'm just saying plot isn't your strong point, so take someone else's plot and do what you're good at, scene and dialogue."

"I have a plot."

"Do it for the next book then."

"Next book! What's wrong with the one I'm writing?"

"Rebecca, I'm trying to help you."

"I hate it when you do that," I said. "I'm knee-deep in a project and you tell me to write a different one. It's like handing me a volume of Shakespeare and saying, 'Hey, why don't you write like this guy?' "

Silence.

I could feel a wave of frustration rising in my throat. It had been a stressful week, both of us trying to work and get ready for the trip, both of our projects taking longer than we thought they should.

"I have a request," I said. "Can you just try for the next four days to be aware of how often you correct the way I do things?"

"Okay," he said.

"And can you say something nice to me?" I said. I meant it to be a little funny, but then I got teary. I had no idea how upset I was, which is the scary thing about marriage or relationships in general. You can go along thinking everything is fine and then suddenly it's not.

Tommy was quiet, which made me feel worse. Is it that hard to come up with something nice, I thought. "You're pretty" is always a safe bet.

"It's just that I almost never get a chance to talk to you anymore," Tommy said.

"But you *do* have chances," I said. "We're around each other all day. And then you sit in front of me and I talk and you don't say anything. And then when you do it's about logistics."

"I guess I talk about logistics because no one around here pays attention to them, and they're kind of important."

It's true, I thought. They are important and I pay zero attention to them. I looked out the window. I used to think that we were a Renaissance couple who was never going to fall into these boring clichéd conversations about who is going where for Labor Day weekend, or whether or not our kids should play hockey, or why I want to talk about personal things and he wants to talk about getting the car inspected. I thought the least of our problems would be that we'd argue about how we communicate or how to raise the children. I have no idea why I believed this, but the chemistry of love is one of the body's finest tricks.

"I'm sorry," Tommy said. "I'll try to talk more."

"But what if you can't?" I said. "What if this is just how we are, and it drives us crazy?"

It was quiet in the car. What if we're both lonely? It seems like we spend all our time either working or trying to entertain the kids, and when we're not entertaining the kids we're arguing about how to raise them. Even though we're around each other all the time, we haven't had a day where we really told each other what was in our hearts for a long time.

As if answering this thought, we both noticed the moon, which was gigantic and blood red and hanging low over the tree line.

"Look at the moon," Tommy said.

"Wow," I said. "Amazing."

I don't know if it was that we were tired, or the relief of knowing that we both noticed and loved the same things, or both, but things between us softened.

"I don't need you to change," I said. "I guess I just needed to tell you how I feel."

As if he could avoid hearing it.

"I think I just miss you," he said, which of course made everything better.

We drove the rest of the way much more companionably. When we finally got to the house at midnight, all four of us tumbled into the one made-up bed downstairs like a pile of seals, but there was a bat in that room. We weren't able to guide it outside, so we ended up scurrying upstairs and leaving it downstairs to fly around and with any luck make its way up the chimney.

Transformation must be on the way, I thought, thinking about something I read about bats as symbols.

This morning I was walking through the kitchen and two cook-books jumped off the shelf when I passed.

"It seems like the house is a little more haunted than usual this time," I said.

"I guess someone doesn't like us feeding the kids instant oatmeal," said Tommy.

We spent the early part of the day washing sheets and cleaning up the mess the spiders left in the corners, and then went for a walk around the pond by the house. The water was deep blue and the sun glittered on it like jewels.

"Look at that water," I said to Liam, who was walking next to me looking for trees to climb.

"Oooh," he said. "It's like fireflies in the daytime."

"Here comes me, Daddy," said Dawson, chugging along on the path in the woods as fast as he could. "Wait! Here comes me!"

Tommy and I were friends again, the strife from the night before (and probably the weeks before) lessened by the nearness of the seaside. Later we went for a swim and I thought, I can't believe the whole summer has gone by without any of us swimming in a natural body of water once. That can't be good for anyone.

Later Isabel and John arrived with their kids. They chose the downstairs bedroom and I warned them about the bat, but Isabel walked into the room, found the picture the bat was hiding behind, picked it up between her fingers, and put it outside.

Then we sat in the kitchen having cocktails while John got out the pots and pans he'd brought and made supper.

We were so happy to see them. I told them about the fight we'd had the night before and John said there was nothing like a good fight to make a car ride go faster. "If I didn't have a cold," he said, "I'm sure I would have picked one with Isabel."

"Actually, I really enjoyed the car ride without one," said Isabel.

"That was the best advice I got from Isabel's grandfather," John went on. "Right before we got married, he pulled me aside and said, 'Blondie and I have a fight every day.' I heard, 'Fight every day with Isabel.' I'm pretty good at it."

"An expert, really," said Isabel.

Then we started talking about someone we knew who talked too much, and Isabel said, "Oh, well. Who doesn't sometimes?"

"Me," Tommy said.

"Tommy," I said at the same time.

"That was what our fight was about," I said.

"You're lucky," John said. "That's a stupid fight. That's a sign of a good marriage. At least you're not screaming, 'I can't believe you're still seeing that crack-whore transvestite.'"

"I don't know, that sounds like a pretty exciting marriage," said Isabel.

I sat there, feeling happy about being in that old house that saw my father and aunts and uncles at the same age Liam and Dawson are. And me and my sisters too. The older I get, the more I know about what was going on with the adults those years that we stayed here. That some couples were on the brink of divorce during those bright, hot summers, or struggling with alcoholism or depression, and some of the parents were about to strangle each other over how to do the dishes. Maybe we children knew that on some level, but mostly we felt safe and loved.

John, Isabel, Tommy, and I stayed up late, talking and playing Scrabble. I could hear the kids giggling on their mattress in the other room and I remembered falling asleep as a child to the sound of adults talking and laughing in the kitchen, my aunt Kathy tuning her guitar, ice cubes clinking in a glass.

Recipe: A Good Family Vacation

Main ingredient: a nanny

If you don't have one of those, try these substitutes:

1. Pick one good fight in the car so you get it all out of the way and can relax for the rest of the trip.
2. At least once a year, swim in the ocean or walk in the woods.
3. Invite friends or extended family to come visit and stay.
   Preferably ones who have the same struggles you do, and who are happy to cook.

How to Make a Creative Workspace

*

September 3, 2008

Back from vacation and the children are in school and today both Tommy and I got to work. I'm a little relieved actually. I love vacations, but it's nice to be home and back in a routine. (I think the kids were happy about being home as well. Dawson was practically whistling as he walked with his lunch pail from the car to his school this morning.)

Anyway, yesterday I told my husband I needed a wall. I was trying to merge both the family story line for my main character and her love interest's story line, and wasn't sure where to put the scene where her new boyfriend walks into her mother's kitchen naked. "Look. See?" I said. "That way I can tack up the different pieces of the novel and start to move them around."

"Interesting," Tommy said.

"If I use this one," I said, pointing to the wall across from where he sits, "I can stand on your desk and make use of the space all the way up to the ceiling."

"I was going to use that to mock up the magazine," he said.

"Let's talk about this later," I said.

We haven't yet, but I mean it. I do need a wall. For both figuring out the structure of my novel and banging my head into when the structure doesn't work.

Today I looked at my husband and said, "The problem with book writing is that you have to write a lot of pages before you find the ones you can actually use."

"Haven't you done this before?" he said.

"Yes," I said.

But those were short stories. I remember once saying to my agent that I didn't ever want to write a novel because they were so long. "I think I'm more interested in a series of connected short pieces," I said.

"Mm-hm," she said. "I believe they call those chapters."

Nonetheless, I've finished 150 pages. I sent my agent the first 75 or so last week and she was happy with them and said that they were relatable and funny, so that's good.

And in other happy news, Tommy has finished his business plan.

"You did it!" I said. "Congratulations!"

"Thanks," he said. He looked good, a little lighter than he had at the beginning of the summer.

"You're handsome," I said, kissing him on the lips.

He finished it just in time, because his severance has run out, and now he's on unemployment.

How to Succeed in Business

--- ✳

September 15, 2008

This morning was dark and rainy for the first time in weeks. Normally it rains so much here that I can't stand the gray, but this summer has been gorgeous—sunny and lush and full of wildflowers. So today I almost welcomed the dark clouds. It felt cozy to wake up to a denser sky, with a jumble of sleeping bodies all over our bedrooms. Dawson was asleep in the narrow trough between his and Liam's bed, where he's tumbled so often in the middle of the night that we've lined it with cushions and blankets, and he nestles into it as if it were his own private burrow. Liam was entangled in blankets at the foot of our bed, and Tommy was hanging on to the small sliver of space Liam and I had left him.

Dawson got up first and came in and grabbed my cheeks. "Mommy!" he whispered loudly. "Get up!"

"Oh, look at how gray it is outside," I said.

"It's a very beautiful day," Dawson said. "It's just raining."

He was right. It's the first day that you can smell a hint of the end of summer. I've been watching it happen slowly—the sweet corn getting taller and turning a richer green, the colors of the wildflowers deepening from bright yellow and pink to mustard, orange, deep purple, and red. But today is the first day that I can smell the slight crispness that autumn brings. I can't wait. We all know how I feel about fall.

After I got the boys off to school, I went back to bed and stole an hour to read, which felt like such a luxury with the cats on my bed next to my knees, all of us in our own way purring.

When I went downstairs my husband was sitting at the kitchen table.

"Have you seen the news?" he said.

"No," I said, opening the fridge. "You know I've been avoiding it since we had children."

"The economy crashed."

"What?" I said.

"I mean it tanked."

"Oh," I said, and sat down.

We looked at each other. It's finally happened, I thought. We all knew it would—we knew that there was too much credit, too much debt, and everyone is living on borrowed something. We knew we couldn't keep it up. But now here it is. The room felt still. Outside the rain fell.

Neither of us said what we were thinking, which was that this was not a good time to send out a business proposal for a new magazine, even if you'd been working on it for eight months and had only just finished it. It was also not a good time to have a roof that leaks and a bathroom that needs to be redone and shutters that need painting, which you know because a few days ago you overheard a small child (not your own) standing out on the sidewalk, pointing to your house, and saying, "That place looks haunted." What it *is* is a good time to bang out a draft of a novel so you can get the rest of your advance.

"Oh, Tommy," I said. "I'm so sorry."

"We'll figure something out," he said.

"Of course we will," I said, putting my arms around him.

He went upstairs and I stood in the kitchen, looking out the back window at the black walnut trees, just beginning to turn. Down the hill, the creek tumbled along because it didn't know any other way. In the grass beneath the clothesline, the squirrels ran and darted, gathering nuts in preparation for a long, cold winter.

PART TWO

Into *the* Woods

October 2008–December 2010

How to Do More with Less

─── ✳

October 17, 2008

This is the conversation Tommy and I had today on the way home from the coffee shop.

Tommy: "So we need to figure out what to do with the bathroom in the old apothecary apartment." (This is the apartment next to ours, which used to be an apothecary that belonged to the doctor who owned our side of the house.) "The ceiling fell down last week in their kitchen due to a leak in the tub."

Me: "Right. Don't want the whole tub to fall through."

Tommy: "All the plumbing in that bathroom is old and shot."

Me: "My hair smells."

Tommy: "I think we should just tear the whole thing out."

Me: "Seriously, something smells. Is there poop in my hair?"

Tommy: "I think it's just oatmeal."

So that's good news, anyway. (I'm not sure what to do with the bathroom.)

We are having such a beautiful fall, I can't shake the feeling that we're living in the last days of the Empire. Every day I hear on the news that the market is crashing and we're all losing money, and every day I look out the window and the leaves are turning orange and crimson and the fields are full of purple thistles and I think, Yes, but we have all this.

Last night we all went over to Isabel and John's for dinner and got drunk in honor of the depression. They had invited our friend Michael, who had the Easter party in the spring. "The good thing about a depression," he said, when he walked in with a bouquet of oak branches for the table, "is I get to pull out all the recipes from my old hippie days when we lived on nothing." Depression cooking, he called it. "The first two things you need are a fifty-pound bag of rice and lots of bananas."

(I'm still not sure what the bananas are for.)

We started talking about how we were going to weather the economic downturn. We decided that Isabel and John were probably in pretty good shape because they deal antiques and vintage clothes, something that will probably become more popular as people have less money. Michael was worried that people would stop buying his sculptures, but since much of his market was in Europe, he figured he'd probably do all right. "I'm not sure what's going to happen to our professions," I said. And John said, "The one thing that's good to have in a time like this is rental income."

That made us feel better, and I thought of something a friend of mine who is also in publishing once told me: the thing she and her husband made the most money at, real estate, was the thing they knew the least about.

"I don't know," I said. "Maybe it will be good for everyone."

We can't keep living the way we do—using up all the resources, not paying attention to what we put into the ocean and the air. I wondered if dealing with the economy is less about getting it back to what it was and more about deciding who we're going to be in the wake of this change. Are we going to be the people who throw ourselves out of windows because the money is gone, or the people who find creative ways to support ourselves and one another? Maybe a depression will actually make us happier on some levels.

"Maybe we'll just start using less and enjoying the simple things more," I went on. "Like each other."

"Or," said Michael cheerfully, "it could be the beginning of the end of the world."

Anyway, if we do get to choose, I choose this: depression cooking in a friend's kitchen on an autumn night when you can hear the geese calling to each other on their way south.

"Although I won't lie," I said to Tommy on the way home. "I *would* like a nicer bathroom."

Recipe: Depression Cooking Use-Up-Your-Farm-Share Root Vegetable Soup

I made this recipe up based on all the vegetables we get from our farm share this time of year and some advice I got from my friend Christina, who started Hazelnut Kitchen, the restaurant down the street from our house, which is where I would eat every day for the rest of my life if I had a million dollars. It makes a thick, hearty, warming soup that is great in the winter and also uses up all those hairy-looking root vegetables from your farm share that sit in your crisper.

1 to 2 onions

A few cloves garlic

A piece of celeriac (optional)

3 to 4 tablespoons butter (I like to use clarified butter or ghee.)

Salt

Pepper

1 sprig rosemary

1 leaf dried sage

1 tablespoon cumin

*A bunch of vegetables that you don't know what else to do with but know
    you should eat (beets, turnips, rutabaga, kale, parsnips . . .)*
½ to 1 cup quinoa
1 to 2 tablespoons lemon juice (optional)

1. Cut up the onion, garlic, and celeriac if you have it. (If you don't, don't worry.) If you don't know what celeriac is (I think it's celery root), that's fine too. You can use celery. Or just onions and garlic. Sauté the onions, garlic, and celeriac with butter, pepper, and salt. I use a *lot* of salt. I love it. I don't think it's bad for you; I think it's excellent.

2. Throw in a sprig of rosemary, a leaf or two of sage, and the cumin.

3. Chop up the remaining vegetables—carrots, potatoes, turnips, rutabaga, and kale or spinach—put them in a large pot with the sautéed mixture, and pour in enough water to cover everything. (You can use chicken broth if you want extra flavor.)

4. Bring to a boil, then add some quinoa for protein. (Up to one cup, depending on your quinoa tolerance. Rinse it first.) When the vegetables are soft, about twenty minutes later, take out the rosemary sprig and puree what's left in a blender or with a handheld mixer.

5. Add more salt and pepper to taste, and if you want, add a little bit of lemon juice or vinegar to taste at the end. This is also full of vitamins and good for colds.

 ———————————————————————————

How to Get Your Children to Go to Bed, Part 2

---

*

October 20, 2008

Oh my God, what is it with my children and bedtime? Earlier this week I told Liam and Dawson they were so difficult to get to bed that I had to call the Bedtime Fairy (whose real name is Hester), and she gave me an alarm clock that goes off when it's time to say goodnight and get into bed. If they didn't pay attention to the alarm clock, I warned that she would come and take away their bikes and put them in the Dumpster.

"Where does the Bedtime Fairy live?" Liam said. He was trying to get away from Dawson, who was following him around saying, "I . . . am . . . a *monster*! I going to *eat your hair!*"

"A few houses down from the Pick Up Fairy," I said.

"Have you seen her?"

"No, I've only talked to her on the phone. I'm too old to see fairies."

"You just need new glasses," he said.

Anyway, they loved the alarm. That night they hopped into bed like bunnies and were asleep by eight fifteen. So: An invisible fairy and a clock with a bell in it have more sway than me saying "Go to bed." I knew it. Just like the sign.

Last night, however, didn't go as well. We set the alarm for seven forty-five, got the children ready and into bed at eight, and closed the door. Mayhem in the boys' room ensued. There was laughter, the thump of pillows being thrown, Liam saying, "I'm a bridge, Dawse, do you want to step on me?" and Dawson saying, "I a *big monster*! I going to *draw your face*!" along with numerous other things.

We practically had to go in and sit on them to get them to go to sleep.

So tonight we had a family meeting.

"Now listen," Tommy said. "Your mother and I have been talking and together we've come up with some new family rules about bedtime."

"Oohh," Liam said. "I like rules."

All evidence to the contrary, I thought, but said, "Good. So. It's bedtime, so that means no more talking, and no getting out of bed."

"I need my phone," said Dawson, looking for his toy phone.

"No books or toys in the bed," said Tommy.

"He needs to call France," said Liam.

"And if you get out of your bed," Tommy said to Dawson, "I'm just going to put you right back."

"And if you need a drink of water," said Liam, "you go to the bathroom and get it."

"Right," I said.

"You don't pour it on your brother," Liam said.

"No," Tommy said. "That wouldn't be a good idea."

"And you don't climb out the window or climb on the dresser," Liam said. "And if Mommy or Daddy turns out the light, I can just get up and turn it back on."

"Um . . ." I said.

"And Liam," Tommy said, "when you wake up in the middle of the night, you just stay in your bed and go back to sleep. If you get up and come into Mommy and Daddy's bed, we're just going to put you back in your bed without saying anything."

"Do you know what I do?" Liam said. "I just tiptoe in quietly, quietly, into your room, and I slip under the covers and you don't even hear me."

"I know," I said. "But let's not do that anymore."

"Another rule is you don't pick up the bin with your trains in it and dump it all over the floor," Liam said. "That's a good rule."

"Liam," I said. "Did you hear me about getting into Mommy and Daddy's bed?"

"That would be noisy," said Liam.

At eight thirty all was quiet. Well, almost quiet. Dawson was in there reciting the bedtime rules like a prayer. "Lie down, be bery quiet. Liam, you be still, and stay down there, and I won't be bery noisy."

Liam snored.

Dawson continued to himself, "Dawsie so loud. Shhh. Lie down, Dawsie. Night time. Be bery quiet. Lie down."

Meanwhile last night I dreamt that I lived in a house that had been literally built on a lawn, meaning the floors were all green grass, and I was standing in the middle of my living room, looking around thinking, Great, now someone is going to have to mow these damn floors.

Recipe: Just-Eat-Your-!@#$!-Dinner Kale Chips

Take about 10 to 15 leaves of kale and cut them into two-to-three-inch pieces. (De-stem them first, which I do by cutting lengthwise along the stem.) Put the kale pieces in a cake pan. (I find that Le Creuset pans work really well for this—something about the way the heat is distributed. A glass pie plate will also do.) Add a tablespoon or two of grape-seed oil. You can actually rub it into the kale if you like; my aunt said a friend of hers told her that you were supposed to massage kale before you eat it. "Massage it?!" my aunt said. "I don't want anything to do with it! I *hate* kale." Obviously, this recipe is not for her. Add some kind of coarse salt—I use Himalayan, but this is why we have no money. Kosher salt works just as well if you don't want to be all precious about it. Mix it all together with your hands and put the kale in a 360°F oven for about 8 minutes or until they're crispy.

When you put them in front of your children and they start to cry, tell them that they need to eat greens so their white blood cells have enough energy to fight viruses, and go make yourself an Angry Mommy Tea (page 162).

How to Be a Good Sister

October 25, 2008

Today I ran into my sister Maria at the coffee shop. I was happy to see her because we haven't talked much lately. This is partly because she and Dave bought a house down the street and moved out of our house a few months ago. I was happy that they bought the house, but it was sad for me that they left. I know that's spoiled. When I told a friend of mine my sister was moving and I was sad about it, she said, "Oh, I'm so sorry. Where is she going?" and I said, "Down the block," and my friend said, "I am not sorry for you anymore," and hung up. (I'm kidding, she didn't hang up, but she did make it clear that having a sister move a few houses down the street was not a legitimate complaint. But it's been so nice to live in the same building, to move back and forth between each other's apartments shoeless with a loaf of bread or a pan full of something we'd just made.)

We also haven't been talking much because she started taking fertility treatments a few months ago, and I don't know how well it's going. She doesn't seem to want to talk about it, and I don't want to push her but then all I have to talk about is my kids, the subtext of much of which is "Having little babies is hard!," and I know she's thinking, "*Wanting* a baby is hard," and it's all true.

Today, however, she did say that she just found out that after another round of shots she is not pregnant.

"Oh, Maria," I said, "I'm so sorry. That sucks."

She shrugged and said it was okay, and then that she had to go.

"She's not really saying much about it," I said later on the phone to
Emily, who is finally pregnant herself after years and years of trying.
"At least not to me."

"Me, either," Emily said. "It's so hard—like each month is divided
into two weeks of hope, two weeks of disappointment."

"I know," I said. "And it's hard to say which one is worse."

"I remember when I was trying to get pregnant, there were days I
couldn't even talk to other women about their children."

"How could you listen to me talk about the boys?" I said.

"On some days it was hard."

"I'm sorry," I said. "I felt that sometimes. I just didn't know what
else to say."

"There wasn't much you could say," she said. "I didn't *want* it to be
hard."

We never do, I thought. That's the worst part. So we arrange our
faces, alter our voices, hoping that no one can see the little gardens of
despair that grow inside us. But sometimes I wonder if we should just
air out those gardens, you know? Give them a little sunlight, let them
be seen.

"Everyone has something they long for," Emily said, as we got off
the phone.

I know, I thought. I know.

Later, as if channeling the energy of the whole house, Dawson had a
terrible time falling asleep. First he wanted me to sing him "Ring of
Fire" five times. Then he wanted to have a talk about cookies.

"Dawson," I said, "it's nighttime. It's time for sleep."

"Sing me another song."

"I will sing you one more song, and then I'm going to go work."

"On your bombuter?"

"Yes."

"Are you working on a book?"

"Yes. Now go to sleep."

"I going to work on my puppy book."

"Fine," I said. "But I don't recommend writing books for a living."

Actually, I kept that to myself. I said something soothing like, "You can work on your puppy book tomorrow, Dawse, but now it's time to sleep."

"No!" he said. "I want to *Write. My. Book!*"

"Dawsie!" I said. "It's quiet time." I got up to go brush my teeth.

"*I want to write my book!*" Dawson yelled. "*You are not being very nice to me!*"

Which I think summarizes the way I've felt for a third of my career.

Finally I got him to sleep by singing an old Carter Family song about a woman who throws herself in the ocean after her lover leaves her.

"I so brokenhearted," he said drowsily, and went to sleep with our black cat Ryely curled up at his feet.

How to Send a Clear Message

—————————————————————————————— ✳

November 10, 2008

My horoscope for November says that great career things are supposed to be happening for me, especially today, the tenth, which was when we had our first snowfall. I took this as such a good sign I took the morning off writing and spent it with the kids.

"It's snowing!" I said to my children when we opened the door to go down to the coffee shop.

"It's like when the leaves snowed down from the tree," said Liam. "Do you remember?"

He was referring to a moment we had a few weeks ago. It was a windy October day and the sky was dark, and we were standing on the front porch about to go to school when a gust of wind hit the black walnut tree. It happened quickly, but as it did, all the leaves floated down from the tree at once, as if they'd made a collective decision. It was so beautiful—a glorious blizzard of deep yellow.

"It's snowing leaves!" Liam had said.

"Look at that!" I said. "Dawson, isn't that wonderful?"

"Yes!" said Dawson. Then, "Okay, let's go inside. I'm cold."

Anyway, we were all so excited about the first snowfall that when we got to the coffee shop, Liam told everyone to look out the window and Dawson got down on his hands and knees and kicked up his legs.

"That's my snow dance," he said.

Then he went to get a biscotti and went over to sit at his own table, which he's been doing lately every time we go out. ("I like it better over here by myself," he says, and if we try to get him to sit with us he just turns his back.)

I told Liam the story of the first time he saw snow. "You were just a little baby," I said. "And I brought you down here to the coffee shop all wrapped up in your pajamas and tucked into a sling under my coat, next to my heart."

I could still see it perfectly—the red coat I used to wear that had once belonged to my grandmother, the way Liam's body fit mine.

We had just moved to town and into our house and were sort of coming to terms with what we'd done, which was move to a new place and buy an enormous house that needed a lot of work that we couldn't afford to heat. We were cold and our house in Columbus still hadn't sold, and I had just put my foot through the bedroom ceiling while I was up in the attic chasing the cat.

"We sat down right here," I continued softly to Liam, "and when I held you up to the window to look at the snow, you just laughed and laughed and laughed, as if everything in the world were wonderful and hilarious."

I got a little choked up as I told the story. That was a hard winter, and Liam was such a bright light in the middle of it, part of what kept me afloat. And now we were facing another cold winter, working away hopefully. We still hadn't replaced the roof (although we have managed to coat it so that at least it isn't leaking, which is apparently what everyone else who owned the building has been doing for 150 years).

"I so funny," said Liam, leaning into me.

Then he turned around and called his brother a jackack.

I sighed. He started this a few days ago, when he was in the car with Tommy.

"Hey," he said. "Look at that jackack!"

"Where did you hear that?" Tommy said.

"Aunt Maria," Liam said. "She was driving and a car pulled out in front of her and she said it."

"Oh," Tommy said. "So she calls people jackacks when she's driving?"

"Yes," Liam said. "She said it the other day when we were walking on the sidewalk too."

"I never thought I'd have to scold anyone other than my wife for swearing in front of the children," Tommy said later.

"And she said someone in the parking lot was an asphalt," Liam added helpfully.

"Sorry," Maria said when I told her. "I just want you to know that the person on the sidewalk really deserved it."

For some reason this reminded me of a story one of my mother's friends once told me, about someone's husband coming home and his daughter saying, "Daddy, if you don't tie your goddamn shoes, I'm going to pop you one." And he knew his wife had had a bad day.

Anyway, the first snowfall! All of us jackacks are very excited and had a wonderful day.

How to Say What You Really Think

--- ✳

November 28, 2008

On Thanksgiving my sister's husband Dave called to see if he and my sister could have one of my eggs.

"You don't have to answer right away," he said. "I'm just putting that in your ear."

"No pun intended, I hope," I said.

"Right," said Dave. "I'm thinking that unless you really want to say absolutely no right now we should still see Teresa tomorrow?" he continued.

"Good idea," I said.

Teresa is the family counselor my sister and I went to see the year we did couples' therapy. She is also the counselor my family sees every few years when we have something especially hard and equally mundane to discuss: the way my father and sister talk to each other, the resentment I feel toward my mother's volunteer work for the library and the peace and social justice committee, when she chooses it over things like her health or my birthday dinner. Or when my little sister comes to town. Emily likes to do a family therapy session at the beginning of her visits. Her reasoning, which I think is pretty smart, is that we get along well until around day five, when everyone starts getting on each other's nerves and there's some kind of fight. So why not have a session right away, get all the crap processed, and then have a more fully enjoyable visit? It turned out to be a brilliant plan. We did it twice and it really did make us enjoy each other more fully during her visit. We stopped after a while, though—partly because it worked and the visits got much easier, and partly because Emily got tired of me and Mom sort of rolling our eyes and saying, "Emily's coming, get ready for therapy."

I hung up the phone and thought about giving my sister one of my own eggs. At first I thought, of course, why not? I'm not using them. She can have as many as she wants. Call me the Easter Bunny!

But the more I thought about it, the more complicated it seemed. I don't know what it would feel like looking at her with a baby that is genetically half mine. Maria and I have enough problems. We can still get into a fight over something as simple as the way I do laundry. And what do you tell the baby? How do you separate your own feelings out if you know the child is partly yours, but not really?

"They recommend you go through someone you know," said my mother later when she called to ask about coming over for dinner next Thursday. Then she added that everyone she knew for whom it had worked out well had had an anonymous donor.

That night I lay in bed thinking about it. What if her body is rejecting pregnancy because a pregnancy would be too hard on it? Maria takes medication for depression and talks about being tired a lot. What if I do this and it ends up hurting her? And I'd have to take hormone shots, which probably wouldn't be good for the people I live with. What if I can't look at the child without feeling like it's mine? What if I say no and it turns out that it's her only chance?

What if, what if, what if. What if I just lie down and be quiet? Brain so loud.

So the therapy session was today and I told Maria that I wanted to give her an egg, but I was worried that her body might not be up for a pregnancy. I thought this was such a terrible thing to say, unspeakable, really, but Maria said she'd heard it before and she knew it came from a place of concern but that my worry was kind of suffocating. (Isn't that always the way it goes? You say the terrible, shameful thing you think you've been really good at hiding and everyone's like, "I know that already.")

"But are you going to go off antidepressants when you're pregnant?" I said. "Are you going to stop drinking?"

"That isn't your business," she said.

"Do you know how exhausting pregnancy is?" I went on. "And you'd have to give yourself shots. . . ." I shuddered.

"I think you may be talking about you," Teresa said. "It might be hard for you to give *yourself* shots. *You* might find pregnancy exhausting. But your sister might have a completely different experience."

Oh, I thought. Right.

Teresa added that if I was going to do this, I had to give the egg as an unconditional gift with no judgment. And once it was gone, I had to let it go and be done with it and not start telling Maria what she should or shouldn't be doing while she was pregnant.

"So when you make this choice," she said, "be very clear with yourself about whether or not this is something you can do."

"Would you do it?" I said to Tommy in the car on the way home. ("I'll do it," said Emily later. "I don't care about the shots, come out to Oregon!")

"Probably," he said.

"But what if a pregnancy is just too hard on her?" I said.

"I think she just really wants to have a baby, and is doing everything she can to get one," he said. "Neither of us knows what that's like."

No, I thought. Our desperation comes in different forms. And Maria would be such a good mother. She's fantastic with children. She also might get a baby that sleeps.

"Maybe I'll finally get a girl, and I won't have to be pregnant or breastfeed again."

"Which shows that the 'no strings attached' aspect might be a little difficult for you," said Tommy.

I sighed.

"I want her to get her child, I really do," I said. "But I just can't shake the feeling that this isn't the right path."

"Maybe that's part of the issue," Tommy reminded me. "It isn't your path, it's hers."

"Maybe," I said. But that's the thing about having sisters—even when their paths are different, they somehow seem deeply entwined with your own.

Tonight my sister called. "Well?" she said.

"I don't know," I said.

"That's fine," she said, although I could tell from her voice it wasn't. "Just let me know."

"I will," I said.

How can I say no to something my sister yearns for so much?

I can't. It would be ridiculous.

How to Be a Good Caretaker

⁂

December 1, 2008

I can't wait until the effects of this new moon are over! Today was supposed to be an especially treacherous day according to my horoscope, and sure enough, three of us fell down. I slipped on some ice in front of the Masonic Lodge and landed on my hip, on top of my computer. Dawson fell down on the way into school. And my mother fell down at a fund-raiser for Afghan schoolgirls and nearly broke her neck.

I was in my study when she called. "Are you coming into town anytime soon?"

"No," I said. She sounded terrible.

"Tommy said you were coming down this morning."

"Not until three o'clock," I said. "What's going on?"

"Well . . ." There was a long pause. "I fell down."

"Oh, Mom," I said. I started looking for my car keys, thinking about the times my mother has fallen, when she hurt her side and was in bed for a week, or when she fell out of a safari truck in Africa and probably had a concussion (which she ignored). "Do you need to go to the hospital?"

"I just—" she said. She sounded like she was in shock. "I think I might need some help."

I was already putting on my coat.

On the way downtown I kept thinking about how rarely I hear her say those words, "I might need some help." Then I thought about how the first thing she did was ask me if I was going to be in town and that I had felt compelled to argue with her, even though I knew something was wrong. Why are we like that? Why is it so hard for her to ask me for help, and why is it so hard for me to say yes when that's all I want to do?

I drove fast through yellow lights, the part of me that likes to be right feeling vindicated, like, "See? I *told* you you need to stop doing so much." But who wants to be right about having a parent get hurt? It's like the time Tommy had appendicitis right before Dawson was due, and I drove him to the emergency room at two in the morning saying, "I *knew* I'd have to have this baby alone." Honestly. Yay me! I'm right! I'll be alone forever, just like I said!

When I got to the Women's Community Building, my mother was sitting on a plastic chair next to her friend Ginny.

"We've been taking good care of her," Ginny said. "You know how much we all love Barb."

Everyone loves my mother. "You're Barbara's daughter?" I hear all the time. "I love your mother!" "Your mother saved my life when I was going through my divorce." "Your mother is the reason I am no longer in jail." "Your mother is a saint. An angel!"

"*Tu madre,*" said a Santeria priest my parents met on a Caribbean island. He brought his fingers to his mouth and blew a kiss, as if he couldn't even describe her perfection.

"I know," I said.

"Are you sure you don't want to go to the hospital?" I said, as I helped her to the car.

"No," she said. "I just want to go home."

I buckled her in and got into the driver's seat. It didn't *seem* like anything was broken. I considered taking her to the hospital anyway, but she'd said pretty firmly that she wanted to go home and she's extraordinarily stubborn, so I did what I was told.

"This fall was the worst one I've had in a long time," Mom said. "I couldn't move at first and I thought, I've broken my neck. But I can move it now, so I guess it's all right."

I guess, I thought.

We started talking about the things for sale at the fund-raiser and how nice they were. Then because our favorite thing to do together next to talking about other people's mental disorders is to talk about other people in our family, I told her about the therapy session we'd had with Maria and Dave and about me giving her an egg. Mom said she was glad that we'd had that session because she'd been worried about Maria, too, that the fertility treatments might be too hard on her body.

"Why is it that you can say that and that's fine, but when I say that she gets mad at me?" I said.

"It might be the *way* you say it," Mom said.

Oh, that old chestnut, I thought. Fine.

We got to the house and Mom didn't want my help getting her inside, so I waited until she got herself settled into her favorite chair by the stove and then I got her a blanket and built a fire. I gave her the phone to call Dad, who was at the community college taking a class on Photoshop, which was driving him crazy. (He hates technology and is used to developing his own film in a darkroom.) I didn't know what else to do, so I put clean sheets on her bed and made it up nicely.

"No, you don't have to come home," Mom said to Dad on the phone. "Becky's here, and the ibuprofen's kicking in."

I went into the kitchen to get some water and realized my hands were shaking. Mom hung up the phone.

"Do you want water, Mom?" I said.

"No, thanks," she said.

"Is Dad coming home soon?"

"What? No, of course not," said Mom. "I told him I was fine."

"Mom," I said. "What if you fall asleep and you have a concussion? I'm not leaving."

"Go home. I'm fine. Don't worry about me."

"I'm going to stay," I said.

"Go," she said, "I need this box taken back to the rug sale."

I sighed.

I remembered something one of Mom's good friends, a dairy farmer, once said about taking care of all those cows and a farm. "It's hard work, but who said life should be easy? All we're here to do is love and help each other. That's all."

That's true, I thought now. All we're here to do is love and help each other. And *some* people, I thought, looking at my mother, sitting in her chair under a pool of light from her lamp, her reading glasses on, wanting me to leave, are *very hard* to help.

"Good-bye," I said picking up the box. "I hope you don't fall asleep and go into a coma while I'm gone."

"Good-bye," said my mother.

"Are you sure you don't want me to stay?" I said, kissing her on the top of the head.

"I'm fine, Becky," she said. "Go home and stop worrying."

Easy for you to say, I thought. Go home and stop worrying. Fine. Why don't I just go home and grow a tail while I'm at it?

"The problem is we've reached the age where they're both getting frailer," Emily said later when I called to fill her in.

"I know," I said. "And I think as hard as it is for us, it's even harder for them to make the shift to seeing us as possible caretakers."

"Actually," Emily said, "when I talked to her yesterday she said you took great care of her."

"Really?" I said. "I didn't do anything."

"You made the bed," Emily said. "She said it felt so good to get into it later after Dad got home."

That was it? That was all I had to do? Make the bed?

Maybe the real problem is, I thought later, that the kind of help we want to give might not always be the kind of help other people want or need. I get attached to swooping in and saving people by rushing them to the hospital or dropping everything and spending the night with them if they're having a bad time. And maybe sometimes that's good, but most of the time it's probably enough to show up, take them to a movie, or change the sheets. Or just sit still and listen.

"That's a relief," I said. "I kept feeling like I should have stayed with her."

"She wasn't alone for long," Emily said. "I guess Dad came home right after you left." He hadn't seen the point in listening to her either.

How to Give the Perfect Gift

*

December 15, 2008

Yesterday I decided that it would be ridiculous for me not to give my sister an egg, so I called her up to tell her the news.

"Hi," I said. "You can have my eggs. Merry Christmas!"

"Thanks," she said, "but you're too old."

"*What?*" I said. "I'm only forty!"

"I just talked to someone at the clinic yesterday. They don't want to take anyone over the age of twenty-eight."

"That's absurd. My eggs are perfectly healthy. I had Dawson when I was thirty-eight and he's fine."

Dawson was in the living room, banging his head on the heating duct. "What are you doing, Dawse?" Tommy was saying.

"I just making noise with my head," Dawson said.

"I guess it messes up their success rates if they take more 'mature' eggs," Maria said.

"What about Emily?" I said.

"She's too old, too," said Maria.

"Fuckers," I said. Then, "Mature eggs. That's so *insulting!*"

She laughed and then there was a long pause.

"I just wish I'd gotten married sooner," she said sadly. "You know?

What was I doing, with all of those good years? Did I just think I could always do this?"

I thought of that time last summer when Liam lost his balloon, his grief as he watched it float farther and farther away from him. I felt that same sad helplessness, listening to my sister as she watched a dream of hers slip out of her grasp.

"I'm so sorry," I said. "If I could have one for you, I would."

"No you wouldn't," she said. "You hate being pregnant."

"That's true," I sighed. "But maybe someone else will."

We got off the phone, and I sat for a minute in the kitchen, feeling blue.

What I meant to say, I thought later, was that if I could lift this pain from you, I would. I would be happy to have it for a while, if it would give you some relief.

How to Know When to Move On

————————————————————————————— ✳

December 22, 2008

Yesterday, given the state of things and the economy and the solstice as a time to think about bringing in the light, Tommy and I sat down and came up with Plan C. We were following the advice we'd gotten from Teresa, who said that when both partners in a couple feel like they're doing everything, sometimes it's good to sit down alone and come up with a wish list for how you would like the next few months to look in a perfect world, if you didn't have to think about anyone but yourself.

I think the point of the exercise is that if you put things down on paper and say them out loud, sometimes your secret wishes seem much more reasonable or attainable than they do when you keep them inside or let other people influence your desires or needs.

I said that in a perfect world, I would want to have the next three months to really clear space for finishing a draft of the novel. I wanted someone else to take care of household tasks, transporting kids, packing their lunches, and dealing with house repairs like the lock that fell off the door on the downstairs apartment on the other side of the house.

Tommy just wanted to figure out a way to make more money and said he would be happy to be a stay-at-home dad for a while if it meant I could get the rest of my advance.

So, Plan C. Tommy takes care of the domestic realm while we treat my writing like a full-time job. Then I can work on Tommy's magazine with him, or manage the house while he works on the magazine.

Brilliant! I don't know why we didn't think of it before!

"What we really need is a time management consultant," I said to Tommy later, and he said no, what we really need is a benefactor.

Today we had a snow day and the kids were home from school, so Liam, Dawson, and I sat down and wrote a story and then worked on Christmas lists. Then John called and invited us all over for a feast he had made. Everyone had gone to the farm pickup and gotten winter shares of vegetables, which were mostly carrots, sweet potatoes, and turnips, so John made a pork roast with roasted vegetables and our other friends Jack and Sarah came over with their two daughters and a giant hunk of cheese.

Maria and Dave came too, and Maria was in a much better mood because she and Dave had decided to adopt. She had spent a day crying after the last round of hormone treatments, and that night when they were in bed, Dave said, "Nope. That's it."

Then he turned to her and said the IVF was too risky and expensive and didn't guarantee a baby and she deserved to be a mother, and if she deserved to be a mother, then they should go the route that was most likely to get a result, which meant finding a baby to adopt.

"To tell you the truth, it's kind of a relief," Maria said. "I can give myself shots, but I don't really enjoy them."

"A new baby, how exciting," said Isabel. "We should open a bottle of champagne."

"I am *an elephant*," Dawson intoned in the other room. "I *going to hug your face!*"

"I'm really happy for you," I said to Maria. "I think this is great."

"I know you do," she said.

We all sat down and the meal was delicious and the snow poured down outside.

Meanwhile, my cat Veronica peed on my novel manuscript. I don't really know what to say about that.

How to Talk to Your Children about Santa

꙳

December 24, 2008

It's Christmas Eve and the weather today just couldn't make up its mind. Half sunny, half gray, cold in the morning, warmer as the day went on, then freezing in the late afternoon. We were all in festive moods, however. I was in a good mood because it was the first Christmas we were spending in our own house instead of going to someone else's. Liam and Dawson were in good moods because in general, that's how they are, and Tommy was in a good mood because he likes picking out gifts for people. He went out in the morning to do last-minute shopping, and Liam, Dawson, and I worked on letters to Santa. Here was Liam's:

> *Dear Santa,*
>
> *I would like a few flatcars. And more trains.*
> *Thank you, Santa.*
> *Now let's see if Santa will bring it.*
> *Thank you, Santa, that's all the things I want to say. I wonder if you're going to bring Rudolph, Santa.*
>
> > *Love,*
> >
> > *Liam*

Dawson's went like this:

> *Santa, I want Santa and Santa Claus.*
>
> *I want a pink present with a train in it. And I want to have too many birthday presents. And I want Santa Claus to bring me a star. A purple one and a pink one. And I want to have another star like a pink one and to have a purple one and like a yellow one and like a green one and like a song.*
>
> *And a Christmas tree in the kitchen. Thank you, Santa Claus.*
>
>
>
> *Love,*
>
> *Dawson*
>
>

> *And I want to have a train. And I want to have a Christmas train. And a caboose.*
>
> *No, no, wait a minute! I need more! A Christmas paper! Pink!*

"These are excellent," I said. "Santa is going to love them."

"He loves everything," Liam said happily.

We put the letters by the door and spent the rest of the morning jumping around the living room playing a game called "the floor is hot lava," until we all got tired and hungry and the children started quarreling, which was when I made lunch and upped the threats of Santa not coming.

I have ambivalent feelings about the myth of Santa. On the one hand I don't like the way it indoctrinates children at such an early age with the idea that Christmas is all about getting presents. On the other hand, to say that Santa's not coming makes a pretty good threat. I had been at it all day. Stop bothering the cat or Santa won't come, don't jump on the couch or Santa won't come, stop saying you're going to kill your brother with your fire truck or Santa won't come.

It worked on Liam, who had been keeping track of Santa since he got up. He's been doing geography at his preschool and loves the fact that one part of the world is in bed while the other part is awake. "Do you think Santa is in China right now?" he'd say. "Is he in Chad?"

Dawson, on the other hand, was a tougher customer. "I don't want Santa to come," he said when I told him to stop saying he's going to kill his brother. "I don't want presents."

"He's bringing jelly beans," I said.

Dawson climbed off the couch and gave Liam a hug.

After lunch, Tommy came home and we all went outside to make a snowman.

"I'll make the penis," said Liam.

"Snowmens don't have a penis," said Dawson.

"Dawson!" Liam yelled. "Yes they *do!*"

"No. They. *Don't!*" said Dawson.

We made the snowman into a bear, which took care of that discussion, and Liam and Dawson decided to climb a tree while Tommy built an igloo for them until it was time to get ready for our friend Toni's annual Christmas Eve party. "Time to go in!" I said. "Time for a bath!"

"No bath!" Dawson said.

"Come inside," I said.

"No, Mommy!" Liam cried.

This went on for a while until finally I shouted, *"Liam and Dawson, get down from that tree or I'm going to call Santa and tell him not to come to our house forever."*

Which was when a fire truck pulled up in front of our house and a tall man dressed as Santa got off the back of it. "Ho ho ho!" he said. "Merry Christmas, little boys," and gave them candy canes and little bags of stickers and pencils. (This is something the firemen do every year and usually I think it's charming.)

"Candy canes!" said Dawson.

Liam just looked at me, as if seeing me with new eyes.

"You still need a bath," I said. "Or he won't come back."

So, don't lie to your children or Santa will come, and you'll have to make something else up, like a giant rabbit who hops to your house with a basket of candy every spring.

Anyway, now the children are nestled in their beds and the stockings are hung, and my parents are spending the night so they can wake up in the morning with their grandchildren.

"We're so lucky," I said to my husband later, right before we went to sleep.

"I know," he said.

How to Organize Your Home Office

*

January 8, 2009

New Year's Resolutions 2009

Talk less, listen more. (This time I mean it.)
Lose ten pounds. (This time I mean it.)
Learn to meditate. (This time I might mean it.)
Finish a readable draft of my novel. (It's due in a month.)
Cut back on caffeine. Coffee, to be more specific.

Well, so much for resolution #1. Yesterday my husband and I had the worst day of our marriage. It started with a fight over the fact that I left the phone under a pile of clean but only half-folded laundry in the family room. Tommy couldn't find it when his parents called to say that they were stopping by on their way to a funeral a few hours north of us, which made him come downstairs and angrily tell me he just couldn't stand the chaos in our house. I got defensive because of the two of us, I'm much messier and more disorganized, and by the way, I *have* been making an effort to be more tidy, which he hadn't seemed to notice. We were about to discuss whether this said more about my effort or what he notices when the phone rang again—this time our landline, which I had taken off its cradle and left on top of the dresser in the upstairs bedroom. So I didn't get to it in time, and whoever called didn't leave a message.

"Who was it?" said my husband when I came downstairs.

"I couldn't find the phone and they didn't leave a message," I said. Neither of us said what we both knew, which was that it was probably his parents, who don't always leave a message and don't have a cell phone.

Instead, my husband grabbed the sides of his face and said something like *"Graarrrgggghhhh!"*

Then Dawson peed his pants, and when Tommy's parents did arrive forty-five minutes later, they couldn't stay for lunch because they'd already eaten in the car. "When no one answered the phone, we thought Rebecca's grandmother had died and you were all at a funeral in Pennsylvania," they said. Then they dropped off some furniture and clothes for the boys and left.

I stood there, staring at the dresser, rocking chair, and bed they'd just left on our porch, wondering where we were going to put them. Every single person who comes into our house looks around and says we have too much furniture. And it's all old. ("Who are we, the Lincolns?" I thought the other day, looking at my living room full of antique this and eighteenth-century that.) And anytime anyone asks Tommy if he wants a piece of furniture he says yes.

"We already have eight dressers," I said, when Tommy came outside.

"We need storage," Tommy said.

"We need to throw things out."

Then we were off on our favorite fight: whether our real problem is too much stuff or no place to put it. The last time we had this fight my sister Maria finally shouted, "Oh my God! You're both saying the same thing!" The only fight we've ever had that was more fun than this was the night we almost divorced each other over which was better for the world—quinoa or meat.

Finally Tommy said that what we really need is to find our credit card application because it's a no-interest one and we've spent the money from my advance and his unemployment will run out soon. That turned into another fight because I said we shouldn't be taking out credit card loans—everyone knows that's how you go deep into debt. Tommy said we don't have a choice, we have a cash flow problem until I finish my book or he gets a job, which in this economy might take a while.

"Then we should spend less," I said.

"How?" he said. "We only have one car. We don't buy clothes, we don't have a television, we only have one cell phone that we hardly use. What we need to do is make more money."

I said maybe we should sell the house, and he said, "The house is the only thing making money!"

Then he left to go play hockey and sprained his ankle.

Now he is lying upstairs and can't do anything, which isn't good for morale when you don't have a job and your unemployment benefits have almost expired.

The whole thing seems ridiculous now, but we were both *so* angry. I keep thinking of something I once heard from a woman who worked in a public defender's office in Ohio. I was working on a short story in which a woman shot her husband in the arm, and I asked her what would motivate someone to shoot her husband. (Tommy and I were still in the honeymoon period then, so I actually had to do research.) To me, the obvious choice was an affair or something like that, but my friend said, "No, that's the root. Usually people get mad about things like that, but when I get a person in court and ask them why they did something violent, it's never, 'He was sleeping with the math teacher,' or 'She took all my money.' It's always something like, 'He threw out all my Longaberger baskets,' or 'He let the dog sleep on my grandmother's couch.' "

Or "She left the phone under a pile of laundry she'd only half folded the day my parents were trying to reach us, and instead of putting it back where it belonged, she got up to make herself a sandwich and talk to her friend Erica on yet another phone."

I'm just saying, if I get shot in the arm, you'll know who did it and why.

And now I am going upstairs to ice my husband's ankle because I love him and want him to feel better.

How to Let Go of a Dream

--- ✳

January 14, 2009

oday we had a good-bye ceremony for the baby Maria
wanted to give birth to. Tommy and I put Liam and Dawson upstairs
with a movie, Maria, Dave, Mom, and Dad came over, and we lit a
fire in our fireplace. Maria had gathered a few things—a baby boot,
a ribbon she'd worn in her hair as a girl—and had found a wooden
box to put them in. She took out a letter she'd written to the baby she
couldn't have, which went something like this.

> *Dear Babies,*
>
> *You were supposed to be here now, to be mine. I will miss you forever.
> There's nothing else to say. No words. Just grayness and a sadness
> that is so, so tiring.*
>
> *Love,*
> *Me*

She read the letter out loud and at the end of it her voice broke
and she sat on the couch and cried while Dave quietly stroked her
hair.

Outside the sky was heavy and cloudy and the wind blew, rattling our old front windows.

After a while, Tommy told a story about his great-aunt who loved children, *adored* them, but could never have them. "No one ever talked about it," he said. "And there weren't any options then, so everyone just acted like it was a lot in life she had to accept, but now, watching you go through this, I keep thinking about what a loss it must have been for her to bear all alone, and I think it's brave of you to let us see it."

"Thanks," Maria said.

My mother said, "You know, we make these assumptions about life without thinking about them. When I got married I assumed I would have babies and I did. I never thought much about the pain of people who couldn't. And I'm so sorry to see you struggling with that now, Maria."

"Thanks, Mom," said Maria. Then she put the letter in the fireplace and we all watched it burn.

Afterward we just sat for a while. Maria blew her nose, and Dad fell asleep.

Then I made a pasta dinner and Mom woke Dad up and we all sat down to a good meal, which might be the best thing to do after you let go of one dream to make space for another.

How to Multitask Like a Champion

--- ✶

January 21, 2009

Boy, this winter! It's one thing after another. First Tommy's ankle (it turns out it's actually broken) and last night the pipes froze. Today my friend Toni left a message on our machine that said something like, "Hey, Becky. I heard from your mom that Tommy broke his ankle. Let me know if there's anything we can help you with."

I called her back. "Can you help me be nicer to the people I live with?" I said. The furnace had quit the night before and I had just spent the last half hour in the crawl space in the basement with a hair dryer trying to unfreeze some pipes, hoping that the warm air I was blowing into the dark corners wasn't waking up any hibernating black snakes.

Oh dear. I've been trying not to feel overwhelmed and to be kind to my sweet husband with his broken ankle, but this morning I woke up with a headache and a cold house, and when I was downstairs in the kitchen making the kids breakfast in a down parka, I just got mad at everyone. I know none of this is anyone's fault. I know the idea is to love and cherish each other in sickness and in health, but how do you do that when two small people keep asking you for juice and water or to wipe their bottoms, and one big person keeps saying things like, "Can you bring me that glass?" "Can you bring in the recycling?" "Can you get into that crawl space in the basement?"

Sigh. I don't think I used to be this angry. I think I know many mothers with boys ages two and four who don't seem furious all the time. What is their secret? Valium?

Toni pointed out that since Tommy and I had a Quaker ceremony and wrote our own vows, I didn't actually promise to cherish anyone in sickness and in health.

"That's right," I said. "I think I just said something about him making me a nicer person."

"Ha ha ha," we both said, and then she said, "Well, we're here for you. Call us if you need groceries," which was very, very nice.

"Thank you," I said, hanging up the phone.

Anyway, I got the pipes unfrozen and Tommy went to the store himself and got new filters for the furnace and some food, largely because it was easier to shop on crutches than to be in the house with me and my rage.

I made a roast chicken, played Chutes and Ladders with the kids, and talked to Isabel on the phone. ("Don't worry," she said. "John and I had a huge fight this morning over a pen.") By the time Tommy came home I was feeling much better.

"How was it?" I said, after I apologized for being such a crab all morning.

"Not bad," he said. "I got to ride on one of those electric scooters."

Later he went out to go watch the team he used to be a part of play hockey and I put the children to bed.

I was drawing them a bath when Emily called, wanting to know what labor felt like. Her baby is due in two weeks and she'd been having cramps for about twelve hours.

"That could be labor," I said. "Oh, that's so exciting!"

How is it that in the face of all the frustration of being a parent, in the face of what it does to our self-esteem and how it challenges our marriages, our hearts still lift at the thought of a new baby? It's amazing. I think it's that somewhere in the back of all this we know that children deepen our lives even as raising them tests everything else.

I was standing there with the phone wedged between my ear and my shoulder talking to my sister about whether or not Mom and Dad would get there in time since they are traveling by train when I looked up to see if the boys were getting into the tub. Dawson was standing by the sink wearing no pants, a sweater, and knee-high rubber boots and saying loudly, "*I am an alligator!* Do you want to come to my party?"

Liam was naked and peeing into the bathtub.

"*I going to bite you up!*" Dawson yelled.

"That is *not* a good party!" Liam said.

"You will not believe this," I said to my sister. I described the scene to her and we both started laughing.

"I'd better go," I said. "I'll call you back when they're in bed."

"Tonight I have a potluck dinner to go to," she said, "but I'll be around tomorrow."

Not if you're in labor, I thought, but I kept that to myself. I hosted a graduation party at my house the night that I went into labor with Liam. You think your life is going to change that little before you have children. You might as well enjoy the illusion as long as you can.

How to Enjoy a Snow Day

January 23, 2009

I t turns out that my sister was just having prelabor warm-up contractions, so no baby yet.

My horoscope today said that my home life would overtake work and that is absolutely true. It was a snow day, and school was cancelled again—the third time this year and we haven't even hit February. The whole day, one of my three this week with child care, was lost.

"How do people with small children write books?" I said to my husband, who was lying in bed with his cast in the air. "I'm not sure if they do," he said.

Luckily, Isabel and John were in the same boat, so they came over at around eleven. John cut down a dead tree in our woods so we built a fire and sat down while the children amused themselves by pretending it was Christmas. They marched up into the attic like a little brigade and got all the Christmas decorations out and redecorated the Christmas tree we'd half undecorated the day the pipes froze.

After lunch Isabel and I went to the coffee shop with Dawson and her daughter Sam. Half of our town was there with their children, parents who usually go to work but had to stay home, all looking a little crazy around the eyes. "Nora doesn't even go to school yet," said the new young doctor's wife, who just moved here from North Carolina, "but it was as if something drew us to the coffee shop."

Probably the angst of parents all over town, needing to get out of the house, I thought.

Isabel and I ordered coffee and slipped into a booth.

"We'll look back on this a year from now and it will all be all right, right?" I said as we sat down. I'll admit I was feeling a little blue. On the surface the day had looked so wonderful. All of us in the living room in front of our stone fireplace, my husband there with his leg in a cast as if we were in a ski lodge, as if we were people who could go on skiing vacations to Vail and break an ankle and sit in front of cozy fires all day. The children singing their made-up Christmas carols in the background ("It's just like Christmas, we're decorating under the tree, la la la. Candy! Candy canes! We like Santa!") while redecorating the tree.

But in the back of my head I kept hearing a nagging voice saying, "I'll never get my work done, I'll never get to the gym, I'll never finish the article I'm supposed to be writing for *Wondertime* on how to survive a stay-at-home day because the kids are always home." (This actually happens to me all the time. I'll get assigned a story and then everything the story is trying to fix happens to me. Once I was writing a piece called "How to Stay Close to People You Love," and over the course of writing it I got into a fight with my mother, stopped talking to my sister, and broke up with my boyfriend.)

"Of course you will," Isabel said. "This is just a rough patch. The one thing neither of you are talking about is how hard it has been for Tommy to have to give up on his magazine idea."

"And not being able to work," I said. I could feel my eyes getting wet. "And we're both such romantics—we want to support each other's dreams and take care of each other, but we keep fighting over stupid things like who put the cat food by the sink, or why it was a good idea to invite people over for dinner again when we don't have a dishwasher."

"And you're both so sensitive," said Isabel.

Isabel put her arm around me. I leaned into her. "I like it that you both believe in your dreams," she went on. "It's what makes you fun to be friends with."

"You always do this," I said. "I think I'm holding it together and then you say something sweet and I just start to cry."

She gave me a squeeze and I felt the tears coming so we left the coffee shop. As we walked up the street through the snow, I kept thinking that before I got married I thought that finding your soul mate, which I still believe my husband is, meant things would go smoothly. I had all these romantic notions about this being the person meant for me, and that everything would be easier for us than for people who got married just because they thought marriage was a good idea.

Now that I've been married for almost eight years, I still think that soul mates are very real, but they're a little different from what you imagine. I think they're just someone from your past life who found you in this one and then said, "All right, we didn't learn what we were supposed to learn the last time around, so let's work it out now."

And this afternoon, walking up the hill toward home, coffee cups in hand, our children trailing behind in snowsuits and bright hats, I thought, not for the first time, that we probably have many soul mates. Some are our partners. Some are our children. And others come to us as good friends.

How to Relax

⁎

January 26, 2009

Now I'm really wishing I had been able to relax during the snow day, because it's all worked out. People have been so nice to us since Tommy broke his ankle. Dave did grocery shopping for us yesterday, our tenant Mike came over and said he'd heard about Tommy's injury and shoveled the sidewalk, and my agent called this morning to see how I was doing (she'd been reading my blog). "I think you need to give yourself more time for the novel," she said. "Would it help if you got a little bit more of your advance, too?"

"Yes!" I said. "That would help us so much!"

So she called and my editor agreed to an extension and an advance on the advance if I sent her some pages, and then make fixes. And last night our friends Sarah and Vicki came over with dinner in a box, a feast of venison sausage, cooked cabbage with mustard, a creamy parsnip soufflé, and a bottle of wine.

I'm beginning to feel like maybe this is just the universe saying, Slow down, stop. Focus on one thing at a time, not a hundred. There are always things to worry about—the economy, global politics, whether or not we'll be able to keep getting work. But right now, here, we all have good food and company and it's all right.

Besides, all the farmers say winter is a good time to be quiet and reflect. (Well, one farmer I know—my friend Evangeline—says that. Other farmers I know say winter is a good time to belly up to the bar and find someone to lie down with. It all depends on your perspective. Which is what Mercury in retrograde is all about anyway, and according to my horoscope, that's what's happening now.)

Tonight we went to Isabel and John's for dinner and in the car on the way home Tommy started singing. I love it when he sings. He has a clear, strong voice and is part of an all-male choir that tours Europe every few years, but it's rare to hear him sing by himself. ("I only know the second tenor lines," he'll say. "They're kind of dull without the other three parts.") Anyway, we were in the car singing "Goodbye Yellow Brick Road," and Dawson, who loves Johnny Cash, Elton John, Abba, and Aerosmith, said, "Elton John! Elton John!" and then my husband was singing and so were my children, and it was like fireflies in the daytime.

"I love that song," Tommy said as we pulled into the driveway.

I love you, I thought. All three of you.

Meanwhile, Dawson keeps telling everyone he meets, "You know how my Daddy hurt his foot? Too much honky practice."

How to Ask for a Miracle

--- ✳

February 27, 2009

It's a girl! Today my sister Emily's daughter was born, after many hours of labor and an emergency C-section during which the anesthesia *wore off*, and when the baby came out she wasn't breathing.

"The baby *wasn't breathing?*" said Maria.

"You *felt the procedure?*" I said.

"Yes," Emily said. "It was rough."

That's the trouble with all that yoga, I said. You try so hard to be present, and then you get stuck being fully present at the wrong times.

My sister laughed weakly and said she had to go. Some friends were there.

"I love you," I said. "Don't forget to take the drugs. Painkillers are your friends, too."

"She doesn't want drugs," my mother said, getting on the phone.

"Neither did I," I said. "But they sure did help." I remembered Percocet making me feel like weeping with gratitude after my C-sections. Every time I took a pill, I'd start writing thank-you notes. I had a whole stack of them done by the end of the first week Liam was home, but then my husband had to go through them all because I'd been thanking people for the wrong things. "The Inglings didn't give us the froggy onesie," he'd say. "We don't have a stroller. Who is Stan?"

"I love you so much!" I'd say. "Look at this perfect baby we made," and then I'd start crying.

Later I called Peter to see how Emily was doing. He was in awe, the way you are when you first have a child. Like all of a sudden the world you moved through so recklessly, climbing trees or mountains, jumping off rope swings, getting in and out of cars without thinking twice, has completely changed. And your heart is so full—you didn't even know it could be this big, and it keeps expanding.

I didn't tell him that it would wear off and you'd have a day like I did today, another snow day, where you want to spend time having fun with your children but instead you argue about everything—who was sitting in what car seat, why you can't turn the gas log fireplace on and off at Great-grandmother's, why we couldn't stay at Isabel and John's for the rest of our lives. Because then I'd have to tell him that it comes back too, when you see them sleeping, or you read about war in another country somewhere, or they climb on you with their sticky hands and say, "We just want to love you all the time," and it flays your heart all over again and you can't imagine your life without them.

Peter started telling me how close they'd come to losing the baby—how when she came out she was blue and not breathing. The doctor slapped her, rubbed her chest, and yelled, "Breathe! Breathe!" But she had swallowed meconium and so they rammed tubes into her throat and put a stethoscope up to her lungs and all Peter could hear was, "I'm not hearing anything! No sound! Keep pumping!"

Peter had reached out and put a couple of fingers on her chest. "Come on, honey," he said shakily. "Take a deep breath. Welcome to earth, sweetie. Give a good cry."

Nothing.

"Breathe, honey," he said. "Breathe. *Breathe. Breathe!*" and finally she turned her head to the side, snorted, cleared her throat, and spat. Then, without crying, she let out a huge sigh.

I was thinking about just how much of a miracle Amalia is. Years ago, before my sister and her husband were married, Emily got pregnant. She made a very difficult decision to have an abortion and she carried a lot of grief around it for years. After she got married, she couldn't get pregnant. She tried everything—diet, therapy, praying—and nothing worked. It was as if her body had just closed up. She went to a Western doctor who said everything was fine, and then finally she went to an acupuncturist who agreed that her uterus was fine, it was her heart that was the problem. It was still too wounded from an earlier trauma, and if she wanted to get pregnant, she had to heal her heart.

My sister burst into tears. How do you do that? It's one thing to heal your body, but your heart? She cried as she drove home, and when she got back to her house she opened her journal and decided to write a letter to her unborn baby. She only got one line on the page before her husband came home and they got into a fight. Then they made up and a few weeks later she called to say she was pregnant.

The one line she'd written in her journal was, "I just wish you would come back."

Recipe: Heal Your Heart

Sit in a quiet room with a notebook. Ask yourself what it is that needs to be healed. Write for ten minutes—a letter to your heartache, or to yourself.

Dear heartache,
Dear (your name here),
Dear body I've been talking about so meanly,

Dear former self who did something I'm so ashamed of,

Write a letter to this person, body part, ghost that has been haunting you.

Put it away.

Go pick a fight with someone you love.

Repeat until you realize you are both on the same side.

Or you can try this:

Sit in a quiet room with a notebook. Ask yourself what it is that needs to be healed. Write for ten minutes—to your heartache, to yourself, whatever it is that comes up. Put the notebook down quietly. Close your eyes and focus on your breath. Try to feel where your grief lives in your body. Is your throat or chest tight? Breathe into it, feel its pulse. When you exhale, give it permission to move.

If it won't move, put on your favorite music and dance like no one is watching for at least a half an hour. Even if it frightens your family, just go for it. I promise, something will shift.

How to Balance Your Home Life with Your Career

—————————————————————————— ✳

March 3, 2009

Yesterday Tommy had a job interview for a copyediting position at a nearby college. Last night we were talking about how great it would be to have a steady income and benefits. (Although happily, we did get another check from my publisher yesterday, so we have a small cushion.) I am a little worried about what will happen to the house if he goes back to work, though.

"The thing is, Tommy's so good at running things," I said today to my friend Sandra, who used to work with Tommy when he was a managing editor. Last weekend I left the house for two days to write, and while I was gone he kept the house clean and the children were dressed the way my mother and sister like to see them (i.e., matching socks, clothes with no dried oatmeal on them, combed hair). He managed to clean out, lightly furnish, and rent a recently vacated apartment in our house, all on a still-healing ankle. And in his spare time he's doing freelance copyediting.

"Seriously," she said. "He cleans, he's good with the kids, he puts out, you do not want to let go of that." Then she added that what he really had was the classic work/home life-balance problem we talk about all the time in magazines: he's excellent at running an office and equally excellent at running a home.

It's true. He doesn't get mad when the boys climb on him, he coaches them in hockey, made their Halloween costumes by hand, and he remembers what allergies other kids in the classroom have. And he can knit. (He learned in college from a bunch of women who lived in his dorm. "It was a thing to do while we were hanging out," he said. "I made a pair of mittens and a pair of socks.")

I, on the other hand, am completely uninterested in sports, and don't appear to see dirt the way other people do.

"The problem is, I don't make quite enough money," I said.

"Work harder," Sandra said.

I *am* working hard, I thought, but it doesn't seem to be helping. When I wrote my first book, I was still going to bars all the time and was living in the world I was writing about. Now, I have to mentally inhabit that place and somehow the kids are always home, either because they're sick or there's a teacher training day or a snow day, and I can't seem to find the consistency I need. And then the characters in my book don't get enough attention, so they wake me up in the middle of the night, saying things like "I don't like the way my story line is going." Or "I think I should be the one who has sex with Linda's boyfriend."

"Be quiet!" I'll say. "I'll deal with you tomorrow." But they keep chattering on about their backstories and how underdeveloped their girlfriends are as characters, and have I thought about writing the whole thing in first person? (Yes.) And I'm too tired to get up, so there I am, wide awake, writing the book without actually writing it.

Sandra said she'd just read a book about the science of being rich and that the secret is doing the best you can at what you're doing and being in a constant state of gratitude. I spent the rest of the day saying, "I'm so grateful I get to work on a TV series based on my first book." "I am so grateful that Tommy's started a magazine he loves and still finds time to work on the house." "I am so grateful my novel is done and it's sold a million copies." It really did put me in an excellent mood. (Although I did feel just the teensiest bit like my great-uncle Warrington, who believed little green men sat at the foot of his bed and talked to them every night before he went to sleep.)

My friend Jack, a former set designer who was restoring the tin ceiling in one of our apartments, says you just have to let go of the idea of having money at this stage of life. "If you want to raise your own kids, have time to be around them and watch them grow, then you just have to accept the fact that you're going to be broke for a while. It's just the way it is. If you want to have money, you have to work too hard to ever see them."

Actually, giving up on the idea of ever having money is kind of freeing.

Until you can't buy your coffee at the coffee shop or ever go out to dinner.

How to Sleep Better at Night

✱

April 15, 2009

I am having a terrible time sleeping. I keep getting woken up at three or four in the morning, whether by the kids or the cat or just myself. Some reasons for this I've come up with are:

a. My kids have woken me up so many times at three a.m. that I'm now programmed to get up then.
b. My kidneys are stressed. (My acupuncturist said something once about this being the time that kidneys go to work or rest, and your waking up means they want your attention.)
c. My house is haunted and someone died here at that hour.
d. I drink too much.

"I'm giving up wine," I said to my husband today at lunch.

"Why?" he said.

"It's ruining my sleep." I had just read an article online about sleep that said that if you have more than a glass of wine before you go to bed, it can mess up your sleep cycle.

My husband just looked at me. Last night we were both awakened at four a.m. by Dawson, who had climbed out of his bed and wanted to play. I decided to try something different this time, since putting him firmly back into bed leads to two hours of screaming. So I just let him wander around, figuring he'd get bored and go back to bed.

When Tommy put him firmly back in his crib an hour later, it was because Dawson had his shoes on and was banging Tommy in the face with a book and saying, "Read it! Read it!"

"Although," I said, "so many things are messing with my sleep, why give up the one thing that gives me pleasure?"

"That's what I was thinking," Tommy said.

April 16, 1:58 a.m. Why I really can't sleep:

Tommy has been interviewing for jobs but nothing has come through yet. I don't know how to help him except get work myself, but that's getting harder to find, and *Hallmark* and *Wondertime*, two of the magazines I loved to write for, just folded. Lately we just don't talk about it anymore.

My children argue with me about everything. They won't eat vegetables. They need to do everything themselves. They act like I'm trying to kill them by suggesting they sleep.

The tile in the bathroom has started to bulge and we want to get it redone but then we would have to gut the bathroom. I feel like we're putting the shabby in shabby chic. ("Oh, don't worry about it," said my friend Evangeline, who also has an old house. "I looked up from the bath the other night and saw some mushrooms growing on the ceiling." That made me feel a little better about the fact that I've nearly made a pet out of the spider who lives in the window sash by the shower.)

Maybe we need to move back to New York. Maybe we need to sell the house. Maybe we need to stop trying so hard.

How to Know What You Want

⁕

May 3, 2009

Spring has arrived, once again, miraculously and overnight. The apple and cherry trees are blooming, the redbud is out, and trillium has covered the floors of the woods near our house like a white carpet.

"It's so *bright*," I said to my mother last night. We had been invited to her house for dinner. "Every year it's like a miracle."

"I know," she said. "It's one of the reasons we stayed here after your father finished graduate school. That first winter, though, I thought I would die."

We were in the kitchen. Tommy, Dad, and the boys had gone down to the creek to look for snakes. Somehow Mom and I got onto the topic of her mother, my grandmother, and how different a mother she was to Mom's sister than to Mom, because she got really depressed after the second baby.

"What happened?" I said.

"Oh, I think it was leaving New York and moving back to her hometown," Mom said. And then she went into the story, about how my grandmother loved New York City, but they were living in Hell's Kitchen and my grandfather was working at a restaurant so he only had one day off a week and was gone most of the time and Mom was sick a lot, so after a while it just seemed like it wasn't a good place to raise children.

So my grandparents moved back to Lancaster, Pennsylvania, where my grandmother's family still lived.

"But her family had such a dark pull on her," Mom said. Her sister moved in after her husband went off to fight in World War II. He died at sea, so her sister stayed for years and then their brother moved in, and they both acted like teenagers because they *were* teenagers, and my grandfather was working very long hours.

"She just got really burned out," Mom said. She would go to the doctor, a woman named Dr. Kirk, and Dr. Kirk would say, "Mary, tell me what's wrong," and Grandmama would say, "I don't know, I don't know. I have everything I wanted."

I keep thinking about that. How do you separate what you really want from what you think you want because society/family/the world has told you it's what you're supposed to want? I feel like I struggle with this all the time. The hostess I want to be, and the hostess I am, the mother I want to be, and the mother I am, the wife I want to be, and the wife I actually am.

"How is Tommy doing?" Mom said.

"I don't know," I said. "He just got turned down at a copyediting job at an academic journal because he didn't have enough experience in the academic world."

My mother sighed and shuffled her cards for solitaire. "What about his magazine?"

"I think that's on the back burner for a while," I said. With so many magazines folding right now, he decided it might not be the best time to be looking for funding.

"Listen," Mom said. "Tommy is a smart man. He's a good father and he has a great idea. He just needs to find someone who can support his vision, and he'll be fine."

"I was hoping that person would be me," I said.

"No," Mom said. "You need to be his wife. He needs someone else. Like Warren Buffett."

"Mommy!" Liam said, running into the kitchen with a snake dangling from one hand. "Look what I caught!" My father followed not far behind, a slightly bigger snake curled around his wrist and fingers.

"Oh, lord, here come the snakes," said my mother. "Yesterday I said to your father, 'Are you sure there are no snakes in the house? Nothing in the bathroom, or in the sink?' I think there were six in here last time the boys came over."

In the car on the way back I told Tommy what Mom said, that he just needs to find a place that supports him while he implements his vision. "The last time I saw you really happy at work," I said, "was when we worked together at *Seventeen*."

"I know," he said.

Then he said, "It's just being in the house all the time. I feel like I have nothing to talk about anymore. Like I'm not a part of the world."

"That's how I felt when I was breastfeeding," I said.

We drove quietly for a while, past the fields of sweet corn and the muddy creeks. Finally, we pulled into our driveway in front of our old brick house, with its overgrown front gardens and the bittersweet climbing up the front porch to the upstairs balcony.

"Do we need to leave and go back to New York?" I said.

"I don't know," Tommy said. "Maybe."

Later I realized that I still don't quite think that's the answer—that just because things are uncomfortable doesn't mean we're on the wrong path. And the truth is, I still don't want to leave here. Here we can walk to our favorite restaurant and the coffee shop. I don't want to go back to a life where we have to make dates to see people, instead of dropping by with a carload of children and plopping down for a cup of tea that turns into dinner. And the blue hills and the green corn and the purple asters that bloom next to bright-yellow devil's paintbrush in the late summer. Or a field of mustard-yellow goldenrod in front of a grove of pine trees? What would fill my soul, if I didn't have all that?

"What would you think of us moving to New York City?" I said to Liam later.

"That's a terrible idea," he said. "I wouldn't go. I would miss our house, and Hazelnut. And the bookstore and the coffee shop and the gift store and the candy shop and the post office. We can't leave."

"And Grandmama and Boppy," I said. "You'd probably miss them too."

"They would come with us," he said stoutly.

Hours spent on the novel this week: 20

Hours spent on freelance things: about 10

Hours spent worrying about money: too many to count

How to Celebrate Mother's Day

--- ✳

Mother's Day, 2009

Mother's Day began at one this morning with poor little Dawson, who was covered in chicken pox, waking up in tears.

"Oh, Dawsie," I said. "What hurts?"

"Everyfing!" he said miserably.

It was as if his chicken pox were breeding and multiplying by the second. When he went to bed his back was half-covered. When he woke up they had doubled. I spent the night spraying him down every two hours with an oatmeal colloidal solution that he didn't like but that seemed to help with the itching. His fussing, however, woke up Liam, who wanted to help and then wanted breakfast (at two a.m.) and didn't go back to sleep until I don't even know when.

This morning poor Dawson looked like something out of the Book of Job. He has chicken pox on his bottom and his legs and his belly. He seems to feel okay, though. Liam and I went to the craft store and bought some clay and figurines to paint and we all spent the afternoon making little sculptures and painting them. We did this for several hours and by the end of it they were just rolling all over each other and climbing on me the way they usually do, when Tommy came downstairs from working on job applications.

"Liam!" I was saying. "Just *stop* climbing on me."

"Happy Mother's Day," said Tommy.

"Will you just take them out of here?" I said.

Tommy took the boys down the street for pizza. "Shouldn't Dawsie stay in?" I said. And he said, "In this hippie town? There are probably people who would *pay* you to have Dawson roll on their kids right now so they can get vaccinated naturally."

After they left my mother called, thinking it was Tommy's and my anniversary.

"Is it today?" I said. I pulled off my wedding band to check the engraving. "No, it's on Tuesday. Oh my God. My kids are driving me C-A-R-Z-Y."

My mother burst out laughing. "You realize you just spelled *carzy*," she said.

"Well, I *am* carzy," I said, and told her about the night before and my morning. "I think something is wrong with me. Why can't I just be present? I try to sit and build blocks. I try to finger-paint, but after a few hours it gets a little old."

My mother was still laughing.

"Oh, honey," she said, "that's the housewife's lament. It's hard to engage with each other all the time—you're in completely different phases. Before Betty Friedan came along we were supposed to just sit around and love being with our children, but then we all realized that that's not always enough."

"I still think there's something wrong with me," I said.

"Nothing is wrong with you," she said. "You have two very smart, demanding boys who are also wonderful." Then she said that Sunday in Quaker meeting she was thinking about the other night, when we went to her house for dinner. It was a stunningly beautiful night. The sky was a pearl gray with sun coming through some of the clouds, which just made the bright-green grass, the redbud, and the early buttercups stand out like jewels. We were sitting at the table having just finished Mom's carrot ginger soup when Dawson crawled under the table and started kissing my mother's feet.

"I *kissing* you!" he said happily.

"It was just so sweet," my mother said. "No one has kissed my feet since I was a baby. It was the best Mother's Day present anyone could have given me."

Later I was thinking that I'm grateful for things my parents have done—the gentle, firm love my mother gives my children, the hours my father has spent with Liam down at the creek—and I know that they're both getting old and I think, What will I do when they're gone? I'll miss them so much. And then I see them, and we're all having dinner and doing things like dressing the salad or talking about work and the kids are running around, and I never quite find a moment to say "Thank you" or "I love you so much." And there was Dawson, effortlessly doing what I meant to be doing but could never quite find the right moment to do—honoring the oldest woman in the room.

After we finished dinner that night, Liam and Dawson ran outside in their pajamas. The almost full moon was pale and bright, and the sky, still cloudy, made the night gray and dramatic. Tommy herded Dawson into the car and I went down to the front lawn to find Liam and heard him making a high-pitched coo in the back of his throat. As my eyes adjusted to the dark I could see both my father and Liam silhouetted against the sky—my son up in the top of a black-limbed tree, hooting up at the moon like an owl, my father quietly standing by on the ground, making sure Liam didn't fall, while in the kitchen I could hear my mother talking to my sister as she turned on the radio.

Thank you, I thought, but did not say. Thank you. I love you so much.

So I'm saying it now. Thank you.

I love you like carzy.

Recipe: My Mother's Carrot Ginger Soup

Ingredients:

1½ pounds of carrots, halved ("I just do it in quarters," my mother says.)

1 pound parsnips, peeled and quartered

1 to 2 medium onions, chopped

3-inch piece of ginger, chopped (My mother says it's best to grate it. "Otherwise when you puree it, it comes out in lumps.")

3 tablespoons unsalted butter

3 tablespoons packed light or dark brown sugar

8 cups chicken broth

Salt to taste and a pinch of cayenne pepper

Preheat oven to 350°F.

1. Combine carrots, parsnips, onions, and ginger in a shallow roasting pan. Dot with sugar and butter.
2. Pour in 2 cups of broth, cover, and bake until veggies are tender, about 2 hours. (This makes the house smell really good.)
3. Transfer to a large soup pot. Add the remaining six cups of broth and season with salt and cayenne.
4. Boil. Reduce heat, and simmer partially covered for 10 minutes.
5. Puree before serving.

Actually, what you should really do is have someone else make this for you (preferably your mother), as this recipe involves a lot of chopping and roasting and takes forever.

How to Teach Your Child to Ride a Two-Wheeler

✳

June 15, 2009

This morning we were getting ready to go out when the children got into a fight about who was going to ride which bike to the coffee shop. They both wanted bikes, and they both wanted to ride Liam's bike, which had training wheels. (Dawson's was more like a Big Wheel.) I tried a technique I'd seen a friend of mine use, which is to present the kids with their choices and try to let them work it out.

"Here is the situation," I said. "Dawson, you want to ride Liam's bike. Liam, you don't want to share. Dawson, you don't want to ride your own bike. Mommy needs coffee. Is there a way we can work this out so everyone wins?"

"No!" they wailed.

"Liam, what if you shared and Dawson rode your bike on the way home?"

"I don't feel like sharing."

"Dawson, what if Liam let you ride his bike later when he isn't using it?"

"I'm going to use it every minute all day," Liam said.

"I don't like you," said Dawson.

"It looks like we can't go," I said. "Is this the situation we want?"

Crying began. Tempers rose. I tried more reasoning and cajoling, and then, I am not proud to admit, I got mad and threw both the bikes off the back porch and into the yard.

Liam started sobbing for real. Dawson thought it was funny and decided he would ride his own bike to the coffee shop. I tried to quell the mix of feelings—guilt, anger, despair.

"You broke my training wheel," Liam said, his sobs beginning to slow down.

"I know," I sighed. "I'm so sorry. I shouldn't have lost my temper. But honey, those are the consequences when you don't share. Sometimes things get broken."

Liam wiped his nose on his sleeve and looked up at me.

"Actually," he said, "things get broken when you throw them off the porch."

We walked down to the coffee shop, a little parade of post-traumatic stress. I was hoping we could put this quickly behind us, but Liam went up to the first person he saw, who happened to be our friend Deva, and said, "Hi, Deva. Dawson is being a jerk."

"Mommy threw our bikes off the porch!" Dawson said.

"Ah," said Deva, who has two boys around the same age as mine. "One of those mornings."

"Yes," I said. "You don't happen to have a bottle of Scotch on you, do you?"

Dawson told the barista, Emily, that I threw his bike off the porch.

"*And* I saw a monster under my bed!" Dawson added.

"You did?" said Emily. "Wow. Did your monster look like Mommy?"

All I can say is that when everyone knows your business, you have a lot less to hide.

When we got home, Tommy took what was left of the training wheels off the bike, and Liam hopped on his two-wheeler and learned to ride it in ten minutes. So. How to teach your kid to ride a two-wheeler: Throw the bike off the porch and break the training wheels. I'm not saying I'm proud of it, I'm just saying it works.

A few days later, we were coming back from the farmer's market. Dawson was slowly riding his bike with training wheels, back completely erect, when Liam came speeding up behind him on his two-wheeler, hunched over the handlebars. "You need a bike like mine, Dawson," he said over his shoulder as he sped by. "You can go really fast!"

"No, I don't," Dawson said, still pedaling slowly along. "Because I am only three. When I'm four, Mommy will get mad and throw *my* bike off the porch, and then I'll have a bike like yours."

(As it happens, on Dawson's fourth birthday, I backed over his bike in the driveway and accidentally broke his training wheels.)

✳ ———————————————————————— ✳

Recipe: Angry Mommy Tea

Chamomile tea
Honey
Whiskey

What? It's good for your throat.

✳ ———————————————————————— ✳

How to Get Inspired

--- ✳

July 1, 2009

haven't written in my journal for a while because I've been in the thick of the novel and by the end of a day of trying to figure out which scene goes where and who is going to pick up the main character after she goes to jail for punching the police officer she went to high school with, all I want to do is watch TV.

This week, however, I'm taking a little break to give it some breathing room. In the meantime I've been making things out of clay. Mermaids, mostly. I have about thirty of them. This started a few days ago when I bought the boys a pack of modeling clay. They made trucks and robots. I made a face, and then I made something that looked sort of like a dog. Two days later Tommy came home from New York and there were eight primitive-looking mermaids sitting on the dining room table: a princess mermaid, a witch mermaid, four Hawaiian hula mermaids, a coffee goddess, a mermaid with her pet catfish.

"How is the novel going?" he said.

"Do you think I can sell these?" I said.

"You realize," John said later, when he and Isabel came over to look at them, "that this is a very pretty way to put off finishing your book."

"You have to go where the muse takes you," I said, although I know he's right. The book is ten months late now and I know I *have* to turn it in in September. But how nice to do something with my hands instead of my knotted-up brain. And I can actually finish them in one day! Yesterday I set up an Etsy shop. If writing doesn't work out maybe I can sell ornaments. Why not? Novels take years and they may or may not sell, but mermaids and cats take just a few hours and they're so pretty!

"I want the mermaid with the pet catfish," said Isabel's five-year-old, Sam.

So, Plan D. Tommy gets a job at Ithaca College, where he has an interview next week. Rebecca gives up writing and makes a million dollars selling mermaids on Etsy.

I'll start working on the novel again in two weeks.

How to Streamline Your Work Habits

———————————————————————————— ✳

September 10, 2009

Tommy got a job! It's in the marketing department at one of the local schools. It doesn't pay quite as much as he was making before—a little more than half, but it's here in town and it has full benefits.

We're all very excited around here.

"Daddy, you look so *good* to go to work," Liam said the first day Tommy put his dress clothes on for the office.

"And now we have *monies!*" shouted Dawson. "Can we buy a llama?"

No, but maybe now we can fix the roof or at least get some work done on the bathroom. We are also, for the first time in nearly nine years of marriage, on a nine-to-five schedule. I thought I would hate this—that it would cramp my style and I would miss having lunch with Tommy every day. And while I am really lonely for everyone by five o'clock, it turns out that I love our new schedule. The energy in the house has completely shifted. The kids are sleeping better (well, they didn't last night, but there was a very loud thunderstorm at three a.m.), the house is cleaner (or at least it was yesterday), and even the cat has stopped vomiting on the rug. Everyone is out of the house by eight, and I am getting lots of work done. I used to hate getting up before eight, but now I'm up at seven practically banging on pots and pans and saying, "Morning time! Everyone up! Time for school, time for work! I made your lunches, here's your breakfast, I love you, get in the car!"

In other news, on Saturday I was sitting in my office in my pajamas working when Dawson came in. "Oh, Mom," he said. "I see your boobs are down."

Then he climbed up on my dresser and brought me a bra.

Recipe: Scape and Olive Oil Paste

(A good thing to make on a day that your boobs are down.)

Scapes have become very trendy in the last few years up here, I'm guessing due to their nutritional value and juicy garlic flavor. (Or maybe because it's a way to use all of the garlic plant, I don't know.) They are sort of amazing things to have in a pile on your kitchen counter—bright green, long and wiry, they look like a bird's nest made out of vegetables. They taste like the freshest garlic you've ever had, but I find them hard to cook with unless they are pulverized, so here's what I do:

I chop them up into smaller pieces and put them in a blender with olive oil and salt. Sometimes I add a little lemon juice or cider vinegar. Then I turn on the blender and blend. And blend. And stuff the whole mixture down again until my blender starts emitting that acrid burning rubber smell. Then I wait for a while until the blender cools down. (I know. A food processor would make this much easier but I can't find the lid for mine. "I think it's in a box in the attic," Tommy said recently, but who wants to go up there? Not me.)

Eventually I get a paste that is kind of like the consistency of good pesto. I put it in a jar and use it all summer and fall, anytime I would normally chop garlic and put it in a soup or vegetable sauté. Once you get past the blending part, this is one of my favorite kitchen staples. You can also freeze it, but only for three months, according to my friend Michael who knows a lot about plants. "It's all the brassicas," he said. "They don't react well to being in the freezer for too long."

Neither would I, which is why I love spring.

Recipe: Warm, Almost Poached Egg Salad with Great Escape Salad Dressing

This is a salad my husband and I used to have almost every day for lunch when we were both working at home. It started out as a poached egg and lardon frisee salad, but I could never really get the eggs to do what I wanted them to do and the lardons were too complicated, so I ended up just attempting to poach the eggs and then mixing them—however they turned out—with the salad, croutons, and dressing. The result is not something you would put on a table in France, but it tastes good, and then we'd feel so virtuous for eating a salad for lunch we'd have a bar of dark chocolate.

Here's what you do:

1. To make the eggs: Put 2 to 3 cups of water in a pot to boil with a pinch of salt and a tablespoon of vinegar.
2. While you're waiting, call your friend Sabrina. While you're talking to her, wash the lettuce—baby greens or frisee, whichever you like better.
3. When the water is nearly boiling, gently crack three eggs and spill their contents into the hot water. Turn the heat down just slightly to a low boil. The eggs are supposed to turn into white balls, but I can't talk on the phone and be vigilant about the water

temperature at the same time, so that doesn't ever happen for me. (I'm sure that if you'd like to really learn how to poach an egg, you can find out on the Internet or in a Julia Child cookbook.)

4. Meanwhile, cut up some bread into one-inch cubes. Tell Sabrina about all your work/money/parenting problems. Sauté the bread cubes with olive or grape seed oil, minced garlic or scape paste until they are crispy. Check the eggs. They should be done. Hang up the phone because you have a crick in your neck, and anyway, Sabrina has to go.

5. Put the eggs in the salad, and pour the croutons and any warm, garlicky oil in, too. Add a few tablespoons of Great Escape Dressing (see below). Mix it altogether. Serve warm.

To make the dressing:

1 to 2 tablespoons scape paste

2 to 3 tablespoons vinegar (*I like to use either cider vinegar, or Unio muscatel white wine vinegar—my all-time favorite vinegar for cooking) or lemon juice*

Salt and pepper to taste

½ teaspoon sugar or honey

2 to 3 tablespoons of olive oil

Mix the scape paste, vinegar or lemon, a little salt, pepper, and sugar or honey together and let sit for a few minutes. (This allows the salt and sugar to dissolve, which I've heard it doesn't do as well once you add the oil.) Add the olive oil. Mix. Serve.

Yum.

How to Finish a Project

✳

September 15, 2009

Yesterday morning Isabel called.

"How are you?" she said.

"Crazy," I said. "I'm afraid the novel isn't fixable and I'm tense and I'm not getting along with anyone."

Then I told her about going downtown to meet Maria, Mom, and Dad for lunch the day before. I was in a bad mood about the novel and I'd yelled at my kids in the morning and then I was late. I got stuck behind a truck and the tape in my head was saying, "I'm so overwhelmed, I have too much to do, how can I be so mean to my children when they're so small and I love them so much, why am I like this, there's arsenic in rice milk." This made me depressed and distracted, and when I was rushing into the building a half hour late, a woman was coming out with a stroller, and instead of holding the door open for her I just stepped around her and the stroller and went inside.

"Oh my God!" she said to my back. Then she said to her baby in a singsong voice, "Some people are just so rude! Aren't they, honey? Just *rude*."

"And then I may have given her the finger," I said to Isabel. "I'm not saying for sure."

"Okay," Isabel said, "you are not yourself. I'm coming to pick you up."

"I need to work," I said.

"Not today," she said. "What would you do if you didn't have to work? Anything you want."

I said something about going for a swim, coming home, drinking wine, and watching TV.

"Get your bathing suit," she said. "You need to step back and take the day off and spend it with me. It's a beautiful day, and nothing terrible is going to happen if I don't bring the coats up from the basement at the store and you don't work on your novel."

A few minutes later she was in my driveway and I got into the car.

"Tell me what's going on," she said.

So I did. "You've got too much of a stranglehold on it," she said.

"I know," I said. "I know. But it's more than that," I went on. "I hole myself up, working and working, ignoring my family, and I somehow can't seem to find the book, you know? When I was writing my last book I felt like no matter how frustrated I got with it, there was something very deep in me saying keep going, keep going. And now it's hard to hear that voice." I stopped, looking out the window, where life was going on everywhere, people looking happy and alive and fulfilled.

"You have two children this time," she said. "And you're also too close to it," she said. "Didn't your agent say she loved the last pages you sent her?"

"Yes," I said.

"Sometimes finishing something is better than making it perfect," Isabel went on. "Give yourself one or two more weeks, finish it up, and send it off. At least then you can get back to your life again."

She dropped me off at the pool and I went for a swim, and afterward we had wine with lunch and watched *Real Housewives of Atlanta*, which at first made us feel superior, then sad.

"Thank you," I said. "I don't know what I would have done today if you hadn't shown up."

"You are going to be fine," she said. "Just stop being so mean to my good friend Rebecca."

I hugged her good-bye. "Don't forget," she said as she pulled out of the driveway, "finished is better than perfect."

Maybe, I thought. Maybe not.

How to Reenter the World

✳

September 24, 2009

I turned in a draft of the novel earlier this week. It isn't perfect, but at least one draft is done! I am a new woman. I'd love to go out and get drunk, but the kids get up too early.

Yesterday I went to the coffee shop, and when I walked in, my friends Jack, Wylie, and Robert were sending texts to Kevin, who is in the hospital.

"*What?*" I said. "Kevin's in the hospital? How did I not know about this?"

"He went in this week," said Jack. "He had some encapsulated growths on his pancreas."

"How long has he been in there?" I said.

"A week," said Wylie.

"You are all miserable excuses for gossips," I said.

"Gossip takes time," said Robert, who was working on the crossword puzzle. "You've only been down here for five minutes at a time since you've been trying to finish that manuscript. You have to sit for a while."

"Rebecca is mad that she didn't know about you being in the hospital because she never listens to me," Jack said into his phone, which was then transcribing it into a text.

"She's always mad about something," Kevin texted back.

I got my coffee and then my yoga teachers Rachel and Amy came in. Amy had lost it on her kids that morning and was asking herself why that had to happen. "You know?" she said. "Why do I get so caught up in the little things that make me crazy?"

Oh, I know, I said, and told her about a time I was yelling at the kids about their granola bars, which they didn't want because I had unwrapped them and they wanted to unwrap them themselves and Tommy was stuck on the toilet in his cast and I said that no one was getting any more granola bars for the rest of their lives, and how later I thought, Would it be so hard just to give them new granola bars?

We didn't have a solution.

Then they had to go and I had to go too, but I stayed and talked to another mother about her blog because it's so much more pleasant to talk about writing in the bright sunny windows of the coffee shop than to go home and actually do it. And happily, today I don't have to write anything, not even my name. All I have to do is return fifty phone calls and make up with my children for being in such a bad mood the last three weeks. Luckily, they are very forgiving.

I finished just in time, too, because today Dawson is home sick.

Last night he had the croup, and this morning I said, "Dawsie, listen. You *can* stay home today, but if you do, you need to rest."

"Well . . . ," he said. "You know, I'm not sure if that's a good idea."

"If you don't rest, I'm taking you straight to school."

"Well . . . ," Dawson said. "You know, you have two choices."

"I see," I said. "What are they?"

"Thirteen and fifty-six," said Dawson.

"Interesting," I said.

"And if I want to watch the banana Wiggles, I can. If I don't, I don't."

"That's a very interesting way to get what you want."

"Right now I think I'm going to watch them," he said, and went off to watch TV.

Recipe: Chicken Garlic Broth

I make a bunch of this in the fall and use it all winter when we have colds. I like to make it after I've roasted a chicken; it's a good way to use up the carcass.

Ingredients:
1 chicken carcass
4 to 5 cloves garlic
Coarse salt to taste
Celery or celeriac if you have it
Chopped veggies and anything else you want to throw in there that
   might be healthy and not as noticeable in soup as it might be on a
   plate (Kale, for instance. Or spinach. Kelp. My friend Rachel, who is
   an herbalist, also likes to put in nettles for extra immune boosting.
   Although she is quick to add that dancing is another great immune
   booster, especially in the winter.)

1. Peel and chop up the garlic and let it sit for ten minutes. (I read somewhere that this is what has to happen to release all its healing properties.)

   Throw all peels on the floor and let those sit for several hours. (Just kidding. Not really. "You are such a messy . . . *mess*," my husband said the other day when he was trying to clean the kitchen after I'd made dinner. I started laughing. "Did you just call me a messy mess?" I said. "Could have been a lot worse," he said.)

2. Put the chicken, garlic, salt, and chopped veggies in a pot with 6 to 8 cups of water. Bring to a boil. Let boil for a minute or ten.

(I don't know if this is part of the recipe but that's always what ends up happening because I'm usually on the phone when I cook; I'm convinced the meals turn out better if I have someone keeping me company while I'm making them.)

3. Bring down to a simmer, and let cook for what seems like days (usually more like an hour or two). Go watch an episode of something. If anyone bothers you, tell them you are making dinner.

4. Once the soup is really boiled down to 1 to 2 cups, strain it and freeze. Makes 1 cup of broth, to be used as a base for hearty soups as the season deepens and everything outside turns to ice.

 ————————————————————————

How to Apologize When You Don't Really Feel Like It

--- ✳

October 15, 2009

Last weekend we went to visit my friend Betsy in Massachusetts. I hadn't seen her in years and was very excited.

"We're going to see my friend Betsy!" I said in the car to Liam and Dawson on the way to Northampton. "Betsy lived in our house with us when I was pregnant with you, Liam, and she was very nice about putting up with me."

"She didn't call you fat?" said Liam.

"Not to my face," I said.

"Did she call you Applehead?" yelled Dawson.

"No," I said. "She didn't call me Applehead."

"That *is* very nice," said Tommy.

It was such a great day to be driving through New England. The leaves were just starting to turn and I thought again of how much I love fall. I said this recently to my friend Michael, who said that the Japanese have been arguing for thousands of years over which is a more beautiful time of year, summer or fall.

"Fall," I said. "It's a no-brainer. It's infused with melancholy." Michael had just laughed as if that said a lot about me.

In the backseat, Liam and Dawson were talking about tonsils.

"I'm going to be four soon," said Dawson, whose birthday isn't until March. "And then I'm getting my tonsils out."

"It *really* hurts," said Liam, who was in terrible pain for a full week after his tonsillectomy. "It hurts *a lot.*"

"Well, I'm getting mine out," said Dawson.

"It's a real pain in the ass," said Liam.

Tommy and I tried not to react.

"You mean a *paint* in the *butt?*" said Dawson.

"I like how he isn't sure which word is the dirty one so he's altered both *pain* and *ass,*" I said to Tommy in a low voice. "At least we have that."

Tommy laughed.

Then Liam wanted me to sing "Down in the Valley," which Dawson doesn't like because of the "If you don't love me, love whom you please" verse, which I completely understand because even though that line sounds kind of sassy without the music, paired with the melody it's heartbreaking. But Liam loves it, so I started singing just the first verse, and Dawson started going, *"Nnnnnnnnn!"* as loud as he could.

"Stop it, Dawson!" said Liam.

"Stop singing!" Dawson said. *"Nnnnnnnnn."*

"We can sing something different," I said.

"No!" said Liam. "I want 'Down in the Valley'!"

"No!" said Dawson. "I hate Mommy's singing!"

"Dawson!" I said. "That is not a nice thing to say. You need to apologize to Mommy."

Silence.

"Are you going to say 'I'm sorry'?" I said.

"I'm saying it in Spanish," Dawson said.

Meanwhile, Tommy submitted a proposal to the college where he works to make a local version of his magazine in a classroom, using it as a teaching tool.

"It's called 'Social Entrepreneurship in Action: Creating a Green Living Magazine,' " he said last night.

"That sounds very official," I said. "How on earth did you think to do that?"

"There was an all-staff meeting this morning and they had people talk about these new interdisciplinary courses they've developed. And I thought making a magazine would be a good fit. You could have students from the journalism school, obviously, and the photography department, but also business students could help with marketing and ad sales, and kids from the health sciences could work on the health section."

"I'm so impressed," I said, "(a), that you found the opportunity, and (b) that you could write an academic proposal."

"We'll see what happens," said Tommy.

I, on the other hand, made a band of black cats playing musical instruments and opened an Etsy shop. Today I got one view, no hearts, but my horoscope says things will be slow for me until mid-November anyway.

How to Enjoy the Night

$*$

November 3, 2009

I love Halloween. I love all the black cats and goblins and pumpkins, but mostly I love it because out of all the holidays it's the most creative one. And it was so great this year. Liam and Dawson and Tommy dressed up like pirates. Isabel and John came over and Liam and David went off together right away to trick-or-treat. The sky was cloudy, so as it got dark the black tree branches were backlit by a dramatic and moody gray sky, with the moon peeping through.

"Look, Dawson," I said. "It's a perfect Halloween night."

"I can't believe it!" said Dawson. Then he threw his pirate hat up in the air and yelled, "Happy Halloween! To *everybody*!"

Then a car full of teenagers with crazy hair and cigarettes and piercings drove by and Dawson said, "That car is from Jupiter."

"How do you know it's from Jupiter?" I said, and he said, "Look at the people inside," as if it was obvious.

Maybe it was.

And now it's November. Our Halloween tree is down, and our neighbors have dismantled their haunted house and put all of their skeletons back in their closets. I feel a little bereft. All I have to look forward to is eggnog.

How Not to Yell at Your Children

--- ✳

November 12, 2009

Sometimes I think I am the world's worst mother! Every day I wake up and I say to myself, "Today I am going to be a great, kind, fun mother. I am going to listen to my children and be respectful. I will be firm but loving if they don't listen to me, and I am going to be calm and quick with a consequence and I am *not* going to yell at them." And then everything is fine until someone does something like pour water down the heating vent, or pelt someone else in the face with a snowball, and I start yelling and all I can think of is that Anne Sexton line that goes something like, "How do we go so quickly from breakfast to madness?" (Actually, that's not the line, but I know the words "breakfast," and "madness" are in it, and I'm too tired to look it up.)

Last week I was upstairs in the study trying to finish an article on how to fight with your husband when Tommy came in with an article from the *New York Times* about how bad it is to yell at your kids.

"You should read it," he said.

"I'm not going anywhere near it," I said. "What does it say?"

"It says it's worse than spanking them," he said.

"Oh, for heaven's sake," I said. "You can't yell at them, you can't spank them, you can't shame them. What are you supposed to do?"

"We're supposed to be firm but loving," he said. "And consistent."

"I *am* consistent," I said. "Every night I scream at them until someone cries or we all fall asleep." I'm not saying it's good or that I'm proud of it, but at least I am consistent.

And then yesterday I completely lost it. Tommy was at work, and the kids were home from school (a snow day already!), and I was trying to get some work on a book review done in the living room because the study was too cold and we were trying to conserve heat. The boys were making lots of noise. Liam kicked over a bottle of water on the floor, Dawson started calling Liam bad names, both of them were ignoring me telling them to settle down and then Dawson stepped on my laptop, at which point I stood up and started yelling, and then we all went to our rooms. I sat there, depressed. I hate it when I yell at my kids. They're so little and I'm so big, and I know it's hard on them and it's making us all miserable. And also, as Teresa has pointed out, it doesn't really work.

My friend Sabrina once said that she'd read the best time to bring things up with children is often after the struggle, when everyone is calm, so later in the car I told Liam and Dawson that I wanted to talk about what had happened earlier.

"You know," I said, "I really don't like yelling at both of you."

"It *was* pretty loud," said Liam. "You could have just said—"

"You should have said it like this," Dawson shouted. *"Dawsie—"*

"Dawson!" Liam said sharply. "I'm talking!"

"Let Liam talk first, Dawsie," I said. "Remember the one-person-talking-at-a-time rule."

We recently established a no-talking-when-other-people-are-talking rule. I can't believe it took me so long to realize that all of us talk at the same time in our home and that was part of the reason I was dying for some kind of a narcotic at the end of the day. ("And if anyone interrupts," I said, after we'd explained this rule to the children, "they will have to go into the other room and sit by themselves for a few minutes." The first person to go sit by themselves in the other room was me.)

"You should have said, 'Dawson, don't step on my computer because it costs a lot of money and if you break it we'll have to spend a lot of money fixing it,' " Liam said reasonably.

"That *would* have been a good thing to say," I said. "The problem is that when I say things like that to you, you act like you don't hear me."

"We hear everything," Liam said. "We just don't feel like doing what you say."

I knew it.

"You should have said," Dawson piped up, then raised his voice to a high pitch, like one of the Chipmunks, " 'Dawson, you should haven't stepped on my computer!' "

I started laughing. "Is that what you think I sound like to you?"

"Yes," squeaked Dawson.

"Would you have listened to me if I'd said that?"

"No," Dawson said. "I don't really like to listen. Can we go to Target?"

"You can't ask her when her face looks that way," said Liam in a low voice.

"No," I said.

"See?" Liam said to Dawson.

"You need to give yourself a break," my mother said later when I told her the story. "You're a good mother and sometimes you just have a bad day."

You think I'm a good mother? I thought. Really? Oh, *thank* you.

"Just do what comes naturally," she went on.

"But that might be screaming at them," I said.

"My mother screamed at me all the time," Mom said, "and she was a good mother to me. She was fierce, like you, so I always knew she loved me. I just didn't always want to listen to her, so I learned to tune her out."

Great.

Recipe: Get Children to Listen to You

Ingredients:
1 or 2 children
1 or 2 parents
3 steps (Or at least it's supposed to be three. It's more in my house.)

Steps:

1. Put the children and adults in the same room and tell the children that you are establishing a new rule.
2. Tell the children to focus. And sit down. And no, no one needs to put "Istanbul (Not Constantinople)" on the CD player right now, although yes, it is a great song. Yes, so is "Particle Man." And yes, you *have* heard of a band called Aerosmith. No, you don't know how many bald people live in England.
3. In a loving but firm voice, tell them that from now on, if you want them to do something, you are going to first ask them to do it. Then you will tell them. Then you will make whatever you asked them to do happen, whether they like it or not.
4. Follow this routine, and if you get to the make-it-happen part, pick the child up and escort him to the sock drawer to put on his socks, or upstairs to clean up his room, or to turn off the computer.
5. If the child still won't do it, he goes straight to bed.
6. Mix. When the child says, "But I never *agreed* to that rule, Mommy," avoid eye contact, look the other way, and envision

yourself as a manifestation of love—a golden beam of light. Breathe in joy, and out joy. Just walk around the house that way, breathing and humming. Then, if no one listens to you still, I like to breathe into my heart chakra and let loose with whatever sound comes out.

"OooooohhhhhmmmmARRRGGHHGGAHHHHH!"

That usually scares the bejesus out of everyone.

How to Handle Bad News

✳

December 8, 2009

W e had another snowfall yesterday and school was delayed for two hours, which made my children so happy they hardly knew what to do. Dawson, who has been trying to come up with reasons to stay home from school (the newest one being that he's having a bad hair day), actually agreed to wear pants. This was a change from yesterday when he came downstairs wearing a turtleneck and a pair of tights and said, "No pants! Tights and leg warmers only!" Liam, who drags his feet every other morning, was outside building a snowman before eight thirty.

We went down to the coffee shop, where Liam and Dawson had hot chocolate and then Dawson told me if I didn't take them to the play village across the street, he was going to fire me.

"It's a tough economy," said my friend Kevin, who is out of the hospital and doing well.

"And this is the job I feel least qualified to do," I said. The other day when I was on the phone with my friend Erica I heard myself say, "Hold on a second. Liam, I can see you. I know what you're doing and I know that you are hurting your brother."

"I know that's not funny to you," said Erica, "but that's almost as good as the time you said to Dawson, 'It's true, I am eating jelly beans. But that's because I'm being quiet and doing what I'm supposed to be doing. You, on the other hand, do not get jelly beans.' "

Still, we did go to the play village and no one got fired, so that's good.

Anyway, then we went home, and when I was trying to figure out how to make dinner for everyone even though my oven stopped working, Mom called to let me know she has been diagnosed with kidney failure.

"What?" I said. "Where did this come from?"

"Oh, I've been feeling tired for a while," she said. "And last week I had some blood work done and it turns out that my kidneys are functioning at about thirty percent."

I sat down. "Do you have to go on dialysis?" I said.

"Not yet," she said. "They wait until your numbers are in the single digits."

"Can you get new ones?" I said. "Can one of us give you one?"

"I won't accept a kidney from any of you girls," Mom said. "And besides, a transplant surgery would be too dangerous for someone my age."

I leaned against the doorjamb where I was standing. Tears came to my throat, but I held them back because I didn't want my mother to know I was upset. (Although as I write this that seems so crazy. Why wouldn't I want her to know I was upset? Stupid WASP culture.)

"What are your symptoms?" I asked.

"I get very tired," she said. "I seem to need a three- or four-hour nap each day."

"I guess if it's between napping for four hours a day or being hooked up to a machine for that time, that's not so bad."

"That's what I was thinking," said Mom.

"What's the life expectancy if you do go on dialysis?" I said.

"They don't know," she said. "It could be a year, it could be five years."

Only five years! I can't even think about the one-year prognosis.

· · ·

My sisters don't think it's as bad as all that. Emily says she knew some hospice care workers who said that out of all the chronic diseases, kidney failure is one of the best ones to get. You just kind of rest more and more until you fade away. Although, she was quick to add, Mom is nowhere near fading away yet.

"Which is what happened to my cat that had kidney failure," Maria said. Then she added that we should just wait and see. Her ex-boyfriend's mother's friend Mr. Bement lived happily for years on dialysis. "I think he's *still* alive," she said.

"I thought I saw him in the obituaries last month," I said.

"That was his cousin," my sister said. "He had gout."

Emily thought Mom should see a nephrologist/acupuncturist in Portland who might be able to help.

"What will we do if she dies?" I said. "I mean, I don't want to over-react, but we'll all be so lost."

"I know," Emily said. "We're nowhere near ready."

"We never are," I said.

"No," said my sister. I thought of how sad my mother was when her mother died at ninety-six, how after the funeral she'd come home and said to my father, "I guess I'm an orphan now." Even at nearly seventy, she felt adrift.

Which is how I feel now, just thinking about what could happen.

How to Make the Most of the Holidays

December 20, 2009

Yesterday was the Christmas pageant at Quaker meeting and we spent the morning getting our kids ready to participate in the nativity scene. Liam was a cow and Dawson was a bear. (Our meeting is pretty lax about the menagerie; in the past baby Jesus has been surrounded by a penguin, a dragon, and a yeti.)

We were running late already and then we got stuck behind a car going twenty miles an hour.

"Great," I said. I always feel like we can go to the pageant even though we don't go to meeting that often because I went to this meeting as a kid and my parents are still active members. But it was occurring to me, as we languished behind a Sunday driver, that it might seem a little presumptuous that we only show up once a year, stick our kids in the pageant, and then stay for the potluck dinner.

"I have a gun!" said Dawson, pointing his finger at Liam.

"Dawson!" I said. "We don't shoot people in this family! No thank you!" (Which is what they say at his Montessori school all the time when a kid does something disruptive. "No biting, Lakshmi. No *thank* you.")

"You're welcome!" Dawson said.

"Are we going to sing at the pageant?" said Liam.

"Yes," I said. "I hope I don't cry during 'Silent Night.' "

Every year when we sing "Silent Night" I start crying. Both boys think it's hilarious, that a song makes me cry, and then Liam wanted to know why that particular song got to me.

"I don't know," I said, and I tried to explain that the song is extremely old, and there is something about that moment of stillness in the middle of a chaotic and violent world that always moves me to tears. (Although now I wonder if it's just that I know what an instance of grace it is to have a quiet moment with a sleeping infant, because you have to go through so much to get them there.)

"I don't mind the chaos," said Dawson, who was taking his socks off his feet and putting them on his hands. Then he began to sing "Jingle Bells" at the top of his lungs with his hands over his ears.

"Why do you have your hands over your ears?" said Liam.

"Because I'm singing so loud," he said.

It turned out that Liam and Dawson were the only animals in the pageant this year but there was a live baby playing Jesus, who was held by an eleven-year-old girl named Faith. The infant, who had dark-brown delighted eyes, managed to sit peacefully for at least fifteen minutes in someone's arms other than her mother's.

The older kids read the Christmas story and we all sang Christmas songs that the pianist played in an incredibly high key.

"Is it just that the strongest singers are all soprano?" I said.

("I think it's the only key Esther knows," said my mother later.)

I tried to sing but my throat kept closing. Across the room were my mother and father, sitting together on wooden chairs, my mother's ample body next to my father's thin one, her hands resting lightly on her cane.

The way a Quaker meeting works is everyone sits in silent meditation unless someone is moved by the Spirit to speak, and in the stillness and silence I had time to think about all the things I've been trying not to think about—that my mom is sick, that Dad is beginning to have a hard time remembering things, that our roof still leaks.

Dawson walked across the room to his Boppy, who picked him up and held him next to his red flannel shirt.

We began to sing "Silent Night" and I sat there, looking at my mother and father sitting next to each other, old and dear and still somehow in love, my Dad holding my son, my mother singing, and there it was. A moment of peace in this chaotic and violent world. I didn't sing because I knew my face would crumple and then I would be the woman who shows up once a year, sticks her kids in the pageant, cries, and then eats the food. Instead I buried my nose into Liam's hair and prayed. Thank you, I thought. Thank you, thank you, thank you, for all this sweetness and light and the fact that we are all in the same place and alive.

Which was when the child who played baby Jesus started crying and the girl playing Mary looked frantically around for someone to take the baby off her hands. (Which, for all we know, might have been an accurate portrayal of the real-life Nativity scene.)

Later on the way home Tommy asked me if I cried during the singing.

"Almost," I said. "Did you?"

"Of course," he said calmly. "I do every year."

"You do?" I said, pleasantly surprised. It's nice to know that we can still surprise each other.

"It's the music," Tommy said. "It's moving. It's supposed to be that way."

Yes, I guess it is.

It's also hope, that fragile, shimmering thing that seems too hard to hold onto, but breaks our hearts wide open when we finally let it in.

drained the life force out of me I had a heart attack,' or 'We take enough antidepressants in this family to kill a horse. Here we are in Belize!' "

Tommy didn't say anything.

"I'm sorry," I said. "That wasn't very nice. All I'm saying is that you can't pay attention to what other people are doing. You're going after what your soul wants you to do. It doesn't always take the most direct path or look anything like anyone else's."

"My soul doesn't want me to be in a cubicle in a basement office working for a twenty-five-year-old," he said.

"We're lucky to have work," I said. "Half the country is unemployed right now."

"I know," he said. "I know. But I should never have quit *People*. I worked eighteen hours a week, made as much as I'm making working full-time here, and went to New York once every six weeks," he said. "Plus we had benefits."

"And you would be feeling like you had a lot more to offer and that you weren't living up to your potential," I said.

But I thought of something a friend of mine said a few days ago. "Do you know how many people would have killed to have Tommy's job?" she said. "You guys had the perfect setup."

What if we've been really stupid? I thought. But it wasn't perfect. It *looked* perfect on paper, but I had two children under four and the traveling was too hard on the family. And you can't look at it that way. We took a risk, and now we have to figure it out.

"Look," I said, "when you left that job you just had an idea. Now you have a vision and a business plan."

"True," Tommy said.

I put my arms around him. "You're working so hard," I said. "And doing such a good job supporting us. I'll finish my novel soon and then I can make money and you can take a break."

"Okay," he said.

"You'll find a way to make your magazine," I said. "I still believe in you."

How to Find Your Dream Career

✳

January 8, 2010

I don't have any resolutions this year. How about quit trying?
Yesterday I heard back from my editor about the novel, which
needs a "rigorous" edit.

Rigorous. Crap. I was afraid of that. The main character is great,
she said, but the story line is weak and the reader doesn't really understand her choices and the ending doesn't quite come together.
Crap. Crap. Crap. I had a feeling this was all true when I turned it in,
but still, I guess I was really hoping I was wrong.

"Maybe I should learn to milk cows for a living," I said to Tommy
last night.

He had just finished a proposal for working more hours during the
week to gain comp time so he could pick up a freelance job at *Glamour*
three days a month, and was now reading the class notes from his college alumni magazine.

"I think this is going to be a tough reunion," he said.

I looked over his shoulder at the page he was reading. "Oh, don't
even read that," I said. "People only write about their successes in
those things. It's all, 'I'm so grateful to be a CFO and for my beautiful
kids, and look at this mountain we climbed last year on vacation!'
No one ever says, 'After twenty years of working at a job that slowly

Tommy hugged me back but didn't say anything. Instead he put the alumni magazine down and went to take a shower.

Later that night I went to a meditation workshop on the power of desire at the studio next door. My teacher Amy said that we attract what we have. So the more you focus on what you don't have, the more you attract not having.

So, New Year's resolution #1: Focus more on what I have than what I don't.

two wonderful, wonderful children
a husband whom I love and who loves me (at least for now)
a healthy body
a curious mind
two parents who are still alive
two sisters I love
four brothers-in-law I love
three sisters-in-law I love
a mother- and father-in-law I love
a host of supportive friends
a great hair salon next door
enough money for comfort and joy
a comfortable bed, soft pillows, a warm house
a roof over my head (I'm not going to think about the leaks, because
     it's winter and we don't have to worry about that in the winter.)

That is a lot. I mean really.

And now I am going to go watch a reality TV show, about people who have all the money in the world but complain all the time anyway. I think I will also eat some chocolate.

How to Keep Your House Clean When You Have Small Children

✳

February 11, 2010

Third snow day in a row. I need ten thousand margaritas.

"When I say 'Don't climb on me,' what do you hear?" I said today to my children, after hearing myself say "Don't climb on me" four hundred times.

"We hear 'Don't climb on me,' " said Liam.

"Then *why* are you climbing on me?" I said.

"It's funny," Liam said.

And I don't know what happened to Dawson's clothes. He was wearing them a few minutes ago.

This morning Liam was dawdling, dawdling, dawdling while he was getting dressed. I asked him to put pants on four times and finally I said, "Liam! Go upstairs and get your damn clothes on."

"You!" he said, turning around and pointing a finger at me. "Stop saying *damn* and *shit* and all those other bad words you like to say!"

"That's right!" said the peanut gallery, otherwise known as my husband.

Fine. But I'd like to see them try to keep this !@#$* house clean all week (the laundry! it never stops!) and get their novel revisions done, and not have a potty mouth.

How do other people with small children keep their houses clean? Never mind, I don't want to know, because the explanation probably has words like "organized" and "systems" in it, which won't help me. I'm looking for a solution with words like "magically disappear" or "and they also finished her book for her while she was sleeping." My friend Rebecca (who is not me talking about myself in the third person, but a real friend of mine who is also named Rebecca) told me there was a time when her kids were small when she just didn't let people in the door. Friends would come over and say, "Can I come in?" and she would say, "No, sorry."

I think that seems sensible.

"Or you could be like my friend in L.A. who used to let everyone into her house no matter what it looked like," my friend Sarah told me later. It was her friend's gift to all other mothers, Sarah went on. She figured that her house was such a mess it would make other people feel better about their own homes, and since she didn't have time to volunteer at the library, this was her form of community service. "And her place was *trashed*," Sarah said. "It really did make me feel better."

That sounds sensible too. "Stop worrying about it" is another good strategy.

So, stop worrying about it. Until you can't find your wallet or your keys or where you hid all of last year's Halloween candy.

Meanwhile, Tommy's proposal to create a magazine and a working classroom was accepted and got fully funded. It's amazing! I can't believe he did it!

"I'm so proud of you!" I said later, after the kids finally went to sleep.

"Thanks," Tommy said.

"No, I really am," I said. "You always do that. You somehow manage to find an opportunity, even when most people would have given up, or not even have seen it."

So, Plan E. Tommy makes a local version of his magazine and teaches it as a class. I help him with the magazine while I edit and finish my novel. By June, we will be making lots of money from jobs we love. I can feel it.

Recipe: Maria's Margaritas (a.k.a. Maria-ritas)

This recipe comes from my sister's friend Holly's mother, "a born and bred Wisconsinite." To be perfectly honest, the best way to drink these margaritas is to have my sister (or Holly) make them for you, because I have tried to make them myself and they never turn out as well as Maria's. This is what she says she does, however.

2 shots of tequila (Keep your tequila in the freezer.)
2 shots of triple sec or orange liqueur (Keep liqueur in the fridge.)
1 shot of freshly squeezed lime juice
1 shot of water

Mix with ice, strain, throw in a few frozen raspberries, add a dash of Cointreau or Grand Marnier, and serve.

(Maria also keeps a Mason jar of this mixture in her freezer, just in case someone drops by at four in the afternoon on a sunny day—or a snowy day, or a rainy day, etc.—and needs a little pick-me-up. I don't know if sitting in the freezer helps the flavor or not. I think it does.)

How to Deal with Rejection, Part 1

--- ✳

June 10, 2010

Ugh. Rejection, rejection, rejection. Lately none of my story ideas are selling. The women's magazines for women my age don't want to hear anything about parenting. The parenting magazines want essays with answers, and I don't have any answers. (What would they be? "Raising children is hard! We should probably be nicer to each other. Help!") And the newspapers all want a news hook, which is reasonable given their genre but which puts me in a bad position because I can never come up with them. Today I got a rejection on a piece I had written that the editor had loved but could never publish in her publication because it was too subtle.

"It just reminds me of the time someone wrote, 'I love her voice, I just don't like what she's saying,' " I said to Tommy.

"I told you, you need a news hook," my husband said, as I slouched down on the couch.

"I do *not* need a news hook," I said. "I need your magazine to be a national so I can write whatever I want."

I sighed. I think I used to be better at taking rejection. But lately I just don't have the reserves. I feel like I spend half the day arguing with unreasonable people, feeling like I'm doing a bad job, and then when someone sends me a note saying, "Thanks, but we really needed

something that was part of the cultural conversation," I get very dis-
couraged.

My friend Erica says that sometimes what happens when your
kids are small is that you don't have the energy for all of your ambition, and without that drive to prove yourself, you're left with your
feelings: of being misunderstood and unappreciated and rejected. No
wonder both Sylvia Plath and Anne Sexton got depressed. No wonder
so many mothers take medication, blog endlessly, scream at their children, or drink secretly during the day.

Or maybe what I'm discovering is that this is a reasonable reaction
to a ridiculous job.

"I just don't know where I belong anymore," I said, once again
moving a pile of dirty laundry on the couch so my husband could sit
down.

"You belong here with me," Tommy said. "Write for my magazine."

"Okay," I said. "But you're going to have to pay me."

"I will," Tommy said.

"Three dollars a word. In real American dollars," I said. "Although
I'd also take euros."

Tommy just laughed, the way he does.

Later I was thinking that this is one of Tommy's superpowers. He
can just hold space for people when they're upset. He doesn't judge
and he isn't easily hurt, so he can listen and you feel safe telling him
anything.

Once, taking the advice of my sister Emily, he and I and Maria all
went to a find-your-calling weekend event in Oregon. At one point
we were doing a role-playing exercise where the facilitator asked a
woman who was very, very angry at her dead mother to pick someone
from the group of fifty or so people to stand in as her mother so that
she could say what she needed to say and let her go. She scanned the
group, the majority of whom were women, and looked at Tommy and
said, "Him."

Tommy got up and walked to the front of the room and stood in front of her. She took a deep breath and let loose. "I'm so, so angry at you!" she said. "You were a *terrible* mother. Awful. You *ruined* me for men. I couldn't have children because of you. You were a drunk. You were selfish. You didn't deserve me. And I sure as hell didn't deserve you."

Tommy stayed still, neither flinching nor changing his kind expression. I remember watching him, standing there, his arms relaxed at his sides, hands clasped gently, just quietly listening.

"I hate you," she said. "I hate you so much."

And then she started to cry. "Why couldn't you love me?" she said. "Other children have mothers who love them. Why not me? What was so wrong with me that you couldn't love *me*?"

Everyone in the room was in tears, including me, my sisters, and even Tommy. Afterward she and Tommy hugged, and since then I've thought of that moment so many times—how brave she was, how much pain people walk around with that we never see. But it was also one of those times where I really *saw* my husband as the being he is, not just the person I live with. And I felt lucky. First of all, he comes from a family whose attitude toward therapy is "Why in the hell would you do *that*?" and he still agreed to come to this event with me, where we just spent the morning talking about feelings and releasing old psychological wounds. Secondly, he can help people just by standing there, just by his presence. And thirdly, he has a very nice face.

I will probably always love him, for better or worse. Even after time is gone and the world has become something new. .

How to Manage Sibling Rivalry

--- ✳

July 26, 2010

I t's so hot. Last night I took the kids to a Quaker sing-along, and in the car on the way home I started singing an old folk song to get them to sleep, and Dawson said, "Oh, Mommy, stop it! That song is all about Jesus and I'm tired of Jesus."

"I love Jesus," said Liam. "He made the sky. Wait, no, God didn't make the sky. A star exploded and made the sun."

"Oh yeah, that's right," said Dawson. "The sun exploded and that's how the sky was made."

"No, Dawson!" Liam said. "A star exploded and made the sun."

"Yes!" said Dawson. "The sun made a star and then . . ."

"No!" said Liam. "A star . . ."

I distracted them by pulling into a convenience store to get lottery tickets because it was ten p.m. and that was the only place open and my horoscope said today was the luckiest day of the year. We won two dollars. I spent it on candy.

Recipe: Midsummer Cooling-Down Tea
(from My Acupuncturist)

Take a whole bunch of dried mint, put it in purified water, and stick it in the fridge overnight. (Preferably in a glass pitcher.) Strain and drink the next day.

This is very soothing and can also improve one's general mood. I like to stick my whole face it in if I'm in a really bad way. Sometimes you just need a face full of cooling mint water to shift your perspective. (I wouldn't recommend serving it after that, though, but that's just me. Feel free to do whatever you want with your own *darn* mint mixture.)

How to Have a Simple Christmas

————————————————————————————————— ✳

December 27, 2010

This year I decided I wanted to have a simple Christmas, but the trouble with trying to have a simple Christmas is that it's pretty hard to do. First of all, you have to get everyone on board and it turns out that my husband and my sister really like to buy gifts. They're good at it, they think about it all year, and it makes them very happy to see that they picked out the perfect thing for the right person. And neither of them appreciated the plan my mother and I came up with to give the money we would spend on each other away. So the end result was that we gave some money to charity, spent some on each other, and I spent days hand-making lots of presents, which made a huge mess in the living room.

(At one point, when I was agonizing over what to make one particular friend, my husband finally said, "You could just buy her something."

The subtext of which was "Not everyone wants a mermaid or cat ornament." Or it could have been, "I'm sick of looking at this pile of clay." I didn't ask.)

Still, we had a nice Christmas and Tommy got the kids a gigantic toy that you move around with a remote control, which Liam was especially taken with. Really, though, what they both loved was the box, which was long and narrow and, when turned on its side, about as tall as they are.

So yesterday I was lying in bed at 8:00 a.m., thinking about how nice it is that the kids, who had been up since 7:15, are old enough now to entertain themselves in the morning, when a box walked by the foot of my bed.

"Hello, box," I said.

"Hee hee hee hee hee," said the box.

"Don't go out into the hallway by the stairs," I said.

The box ignored me and walked into the hallway.

"That is called not listening to Mommy!" I said, still not quite willing to get out of bed.

Then I heard giggling in the kids' bedroom and the box made its way into the bathroom, and then I heard the box say, "Hey, Dawson. Try peeing on me."

I pulled the covers over my head, deciding to pretend I didn't just hear that.

"Okay," said Dawson.

"Did you just say *pee* on me?" Tommy said.

"Hee hee hee hee hee," said Liam and Dawson.

Needless to say, the box ended up in several pieces in the recycling bin. And we had a talk with our children about appropriate bathroom behavior. Which may or may not have been the reason that Dawson decided to wear four pairs of underpants, one on top of the other, for the rest of the day.

Belated Merry Christmas, everyone! Here's to high hopes for the New Year.

PART THREE

Down *the* Rabbit Hole

January 2011–September 2011

How to Be a Complete Disorganized Mess

--- ✳

January 20, 2011

Hours spent working on the novel: 10, mostly going back and forth
between writing scenes in first person or third person
Hours spent rereading original, raw material trying to figure out what
it was I loved about this book in the first place: 8
Hours spent helping Tommy prepare for his magazine course (which
starts next week): 3
Hours spent making cats and rabbits out of clay: none of your
business

Man, this novel! This second round of revisions is killing
me. Every morning I sit down in front of my little statue of Ganesh
and pray for a miracle. Just let me be an open channel, I beg. Tell me
what I need to write.

And every day I feel completely blocked. I love the characters but I
just can't impose a plot on them. And I *don't know* how to explain what
is so appealing about my main character's hard-drinking boyfriend. I
keep writing "He was handsome and made her feel pretty" over and

over and over again, until I kind of feel like grabbing the reader by the throat and saying, "Look, you just had to be there, okay?"

I'm pretty sure readers don't like that very much.

The other night Tommy came into the family room, where I was watching *Real Housewives* and sitting in the middle of a pile of clay, making goblins that look like cats wearing hats and winter scarves.

"You are a writer!" he said. "The animals and mermaids are driving me crazy!"

"The novel is driving me crazy!" I said, and may have started to cry.

Then yesterday Liam actually *bit* my computer cord. It wasn't plugged in, thank goodness, but still.

"Oh, Liam," I said. "Oh, honey, you can't ever do that again."

"I know," he said, and started to cry. "I just wasn't thinking."

I put my arms around him. I know me finishing a book has been hard on them. They know when I'm here but not really here, when I'm halfway in another world. Just one more week, I keep saying. Just one more week.

I got the boys off to school this morning and took the computer down to the coffee shop where I stood in line behind my friend Paul, Evangeline's husband.

"Can you fix this?" I said, holding up the broken cord. I had tried to fix it the night before by cutting it and twisting the wires together but I only had packing tape and it hadn't really worked.

"Sure," Paul said, which he did easily with a penknife and some electrician's tape. "Make sure you take note that your computer was fixed by a vegetable farmer in a coffee shop," Paul said.

Done.

But do I need more signs that I should quit?

And how? If I quit I'll have to give the advance back, and not only did we spend it, we need the rest of it. Even with Tommy's extra job, we're barely breaking even.

•   •   •

"Maybe I should take medication," I said later to my friend Gia. She just finished her first novel and said it was the hardest thing she'd ever done. Way harder than short stories.

"There's no way around the depression," she warned. "You are going to go down the rabbit hole."

"Not if I'm taking antianxiety pills," I said.

Gia shook her head. "The trouble is, I think the anxiety is part of it," she said. "You have to go into a dark place to feel the full range of emotion you need on the page."

That was a good point, but then I reminded her that my book is supposed to be a comedy.

Gia considered this. I was quietly thinking about the number of comedians I've read about who have killed themselves.

"I don't know," she said. "I mean, I live alone, so I was really able to go over to the dark side. I suppose it would be harder if I had a husband. Or small children. And a house to keep up. Maybe drugs aren't a bad idea for you."

Maybe, although in spite of the fact that I love the idea of self-improvement, I tend to get a little annoyed by the notion that I should actually change any of my behavior to make it happen.

Anyway, I was going to work through dinner tonight, but I think I'll go out to dinner with Tommy and the kids instead and work later. I don't even want to think about what could have happened to Liam. Except that of course I do and have, usually at about three in the morning, when everyone is asleep except me, the cats, and the deer who roam through our backyard, looking for food.

How to Behave When No One Understands You

--- ✳

February 10, 2011

Tommy was working late again last night so Mom invited me and the boys over for dinner. Maria was there too—she had spent the day with Mom helping her organize the living room, so when I got there they were both in a best-friend kind of mood and talking about wall hangings and vacuum cleaners and window treatments. I couldn't find my glasses before I left the house so was wearing my spare pair, which are held together with a twist tie from a bread bag.

"Nice glasses," said Maria.

"Thank you," I said. "It's called being resourceful."

Mom and Maria were talking about a writer they'd read about in the *New Yorker* who had moved to the country and started a blog and was making millions of dollars. I sat down at the kitchen table and picked a mushroom out of the salad in the serving bowl.

"Becky!" said my mother. "Stop that. Now look, I made that hummus plate so that you wouldn't sit down and start eating before everyone else."

"I'm starving, cold, and I know I'm going to have to get up before everyone else to bathe the kids or feed someone, so I want to be able to eat while I can," I said crossly. I hadn't eaten since lunch, and then all I'd had was popcorn.

Maria started talking about another book she was reading about a woman who had opened a cupcake store.

"Cupcakes?" I said.

"It had recipes in it," Maria said. "And she didn't even mean to be a writer, it just happened to her. She just wanted to be a stay-at-home mom, but then she had a baby and the book just poured out of her."

I put my face on the table.

"Oh, honey," said my mother, laughing. "You should become a dominatrix. I was just listening to someone on NPR talk about a book and she was a dominatrix for several years and her book is doing great."

"I heard that interview too," said my sister. "She sounded really interesting."

"If you wanted to upset everyone in your hometown with your stories, you might as well have gone the whole way," said Mom to me.

"But I didn't want to upset everyone in town," I said.

"Oh, well," Mom said. "Too late."

"Ha, ha," I said, and then, just to make everyone feel bad, I brought up a story *I'd* heard on NPR about the honeybees dying.

"You're a real Debbie Downer tonight," said my mother.

"I know," I said. I felt pinched and bitter and couldn't look anyone in the eye.

Maria went home and as she was leaving, Mom said, "Thanks for coming out today and helping me."

"Oh," said Maria. "You're welcome. I don't feel like we got a lot done, but . . ."

"It was just nice to have you around this afternoon," said Mom.

Of course it was. They always have a good time together.

"Good-bye, Debbie," said Mom cheerfully, kissing me goodnight.

"Good-bye!" I said.

*   *   *

I drove home with the kids in the backseat, and all I could think was why can't a book just pour out of me?

Why?

In the backseat, Liam said he had the hiccups.

"Me too," said Dawson. "I want hiccups, too."

"You go get your own hiccups," said Liam crossly, and then they both fell asleep.

How to Have a Nervous Breakdown

February 14, 2011

As my Valentine's Day gift today, Tommy took the kids so I could have the morning to work. I wrote for four hours and then sat down to read through what I'd done. It was so discouraging. All I'm doing is moving things around. I'm not making things better. What is it about this project? A few days ago, my friend Sabrina asked me what I would do if I had a million dollars and I said I would give my advance money back and start doing children's books or work on my blog and make cats and mermaids out of clay and be happy again.

In the afternoon, I met Tommy downtown and took Liam to go visit my grandmother and wish her a happy Valentine's Day at the home where she lives.

Grandmother was sitting in the library in a pretty blue embroidered Chinese top and alternating between staring at the fireplace and dozing. In her hands she was holding a big paper heart some sorority girls had handed out earlier that day as a community project.

I went in and sat down next to her and told her that I was her son Frank's daughter, Rebecca, and was happy to see her.

"Nice to see you," she said, smiling.

"Happy Valentine's Day," I said, handing her a box of chocolate.

"Oh," she said, looking at the paper heart in her hands. "Yes. I suppose it must be."

She had faded since the last time I'd come: she was more shrunken and seemed farther away. The other day Mom said that Grandmother had been talking about spending time with my great-uncle Henry, her favorite brother, who was hit by a bus and killed while riding his bike at age thirteen, so who knows what dimension she was in.

I asked her how her day was, and she had a hard time choosing words to answer me. It took awhile for me to figure out that when she kept saying "There wasn't enough air," she was trying to say it had been hard for her to find something to wear.

We talked about the weather and the fact that it was Valentine's Day, and that my parents had just gotten back from Mexico, where my father had insisted on exploring some caves by himself. Then I told her my sister Maria had decided to adopt.

"Oh," she said, smiling. "Lovely!"

My grandmother has a repertoire of about four different things she can say that make it sound like she's following the conversation whether or not she is. "Nice to see you." "Thank you." "Is that so? My goodness." "Lovely." You can have a conversation with just about anyone with those catchphrases, and she uses them often.

She doesn't give a lot back to the conversation though, so I often run out of things to say to my grandmother, and then I end up just talking about people I know, or the amazing fact that we have a black president. (She is Harriet Beecher Stowe's great-grandniece, and this fact always cheers her up immensely.) This morning I ran out of things faster than usual, so I found myself telling her the truth, that I had spent the morning working on a book.

"Did you?" she said.

In the kitchen Liam, who had gotten bored with the gas fireplace switch, was convincing the cook to give him a sundae.

"Yes," I said, and because I didn't know what to do next, I said, "I've been working on this thing for what seems like forever and I thought I was getting close to finishing it, but today I read it through and it might not even be publishable."

It was the first time I'd said those words out loud, and as I said it I realized that it might be true, and something in my throat tightened, then broke.

"And I've been trying to do all this with two small children," I went on, "and sometimes I just miss them so much and they're sitting right in front of me, and Liam *bit* through my computer cord the other day, as if I needed a stronger message."

I stopped talking then, afraid I was going to cry.

My grandmother looked at me and for a moment she was lucid, as if she understood everything. "Oh, *dear*," she said. "That must be *very* hard."

"It is," I whispered, and then I did start to cry. What if I've lost this book? First I couldn't write it because the children were small and Tommy broke his ankle and I kept getting interrupted, but now that things have settled, I've managed to carve out this time. And every day I go into a room and sit there calling to my characters, "I'm here, I'm listening," and they're gone.

My grandmother looked at the fire and I tried to compose myself. In the next room I heard two old women talking. "How did you get your hair to do that?" one of them said. "It just grew this way, I think," the other said. I wiped my eyes, and when my grandmother looked back at me, she was confused—as if wondering who this poor woman in front of her was, and why was she crying?

"Well, I'll give this back to you," she said, and handed me the Valentine's card from the sorority girls, as if maybe that was why I was upset. I took it and kissed her good-bye, pressing her cheek to mine for a long time. "Lovely to see you," she said, and then, "Oh! Do you belong to me?" when Liam kissed her good-bye.

On the way home, Liam sat in the back of the car telling me he was hungry. Crap, I thought. I hadn't even thought about dinner. Everyone was probably back at the house starving. Maybe we can go out, I thought, and that made me worry about money again.

But when we got to the house, the kitchen was full. My sister Maria was at the table, cutting out paper Valentine hearts with Dawson. My brother-in-law was cooking dinner and my husband was washing the dishes.

"Happy Valentine's Day," said my husband.

"I love you," I said.

Dave poured me a glass of wine he'd made at the winery and Maria put a tuna casserole in the oven.

"How was the visit?" Maria said.

"Oh," I sighed. "Embarrassing. I cried in front of Grandmother."

Dave made a sympathetic sound, and I drank some more wine and told them the whole story. When I got to the place where she looked at me blankly, as if to say, "Who is this poor woman sitting in front of me in tears? And why is that little boy turning the fireplace on and off?" they all started laughing and Dawson climbed onto my lap.

I remember thinking when I first got married, Well, this is great, but that's it for romantic love. We'll have a few years of newlywed bliss and then it will mellow out, and that's okay, but we won't have these heady romantic days anymore. But now I think love is so much bigger than the two people involved in a couple. It's everywhere, with family, friends, the trees, the night breezes, and the animals that surround us. And we get so many chances for love, all kinds—romantic and intimate, brand-new and seasoned—with our friends, our work, our children. What made it such a perfect Valentine's Day was that it was a series of small love notes—my grandmother's moment of clarity, dinner from my brother-in-law and sister, my husband's laughter.

And if you looked at the holiday that way, it takes the pressure off your spouse, who already gave you roses years ago, has seen you naked more times than he can count, and whose greatest gift to you is that he loves you even though you cry openly in front of people who have no idea who you are—or maybe he loves you because you do.

How to Get Your Needs Met, Part 1

_____ ✳

February 18, 2011

Tonight at yoga our teacher had us all ask ourselves how things would be different if we trusted ourselves.

If I trusted myself, I wouldn't worry about this project. If I trusted myself, I would just try to get it done and stop worrying about how it would be received. Or maybe if I trusted myself I would just give up on it altogether.

"How do you know what part of yourself to trust?" I said. "What if two parts of yourself have two perfectly good arguments for doing opposite things? Which voice do you listen to?"

"The kindest one," she said.

The one that has the nicest things to say is always right.

This morning Mom called to tell me that she was thinking about me after I left the other night and she thought I should start working on something I like. "This book is tearing you apart," she said. "Stop doing it. Remove the sword of Damocles."

I have to finish it, I said. It's really close to being done.

How to Break That Leaving-the-House Inertia That Sets In Every Time You Want to Go Somewhere

--- ✳

March 13, 2011

Yesterday, a Saturday, we couldn't figure out what to do. We were all restively wandering around the house—starting projects with blocks and Legos (the children), folding laundry (me), doing something in the kitchen (Tommy).

Finally we decided we had to get out of the house, at which point we all fell into that confused leaving-the-house inertia that always seems to set in the second we make a decision. Liam picked up a book and began to read. I couldn't find my glasses. Tommy decided it looked like rain and he needed to check the buckets in the attic. Dawson had the devil in him and was just wandering around pulling things off shelves.

"Okay," I said. "That's it. Everyone get into the car, now."

"I don't have shoes," said Liam.

"Go upstairs and find them," I said.

Liam went upstairs. Five minutes went by. Finally I went upstairs, where Liam was making a cat trap out of blocks.

"Liam!" I said. "Put on your shoes!"

Dawson, who had come up the stairs with me, went into my room, where he found a shoebox full of stockings that he began throwing over his shoulder as fast as he could.

"What the—?" I said. "Oh my God! Dawson, what are you doing? What has gotten into you?"

"That's a dollar," my husband said.

"What?" I said.

"Every time the kids say 'Oh my God' I make them pay me a dollar," Tommy said. "And you swore earlier, so that's two dollars."

"I am not giving you a dollar," I said. "Did you see what Dawson just did? He was like a crazy person."

"Two dollars," said my husband.

"Ooooh," said Liam. "Ha ha ha ha ha ha! Mommy owes Daddy two dollars. You need to give me two dollars too, Mommy!"

"Yay!" said Dawson. "Give us all your money!"

"I am not giving anyone any goddamn money," I said.

"That's three dollars," said my husband, calmly holding out his hand. I gave him three dollars.

"I'll get you for this," I said under my breath.

"Guess you won't have enough for a cappuccino tomorrow," he said happily, putting his wallet in his pocket. Then they all went out to the car and buckled themselves in, easy as you please.

This is the trouble with having rules in the house—I keep breaking them. Like pick up after yourself or don't watch more than an hour of TV a day. No sneaking peeks at *True Blood* in the afternoon, when you should be writing. Don't swear. This is why. Goddammit.

But at least now we know what to do next time we're having a hard time leaving the house. Get Mommy to swear, and everyone will have some pocket money for ice cream.

This morning I got up and went for a walk with Isabel. We walked through the woods and past the town graveyard. She talked about how she and John have been trying to get a loan for their store and kept getting rejected, and I talked about a conversation Tommy and I had at breakfast in which I said we should have been more frugal back when he first left his job at *People*. Tommy said that he'd always worked under the assumption that we'd made money in the past, we'd been good with money, and so we'd be able to make it again. But now we've run out of money and we still need a new roof and we should have done that a long time ago. ("Although it was probably much nicer to go out to dinner," Isabel said.

"I know," I shuddered. "A new roof." What joyless spending. Like buying new tires.)

Then we started talking about this whole idea of trying to follow your dreams and what it means.

"I keep thinking, What is the point of all this following your dreams?" she said. "I feel like everything was lining up so nicely. We did what we believe in, we reached for the stars, and then we fell flat on our faces."

"Oh, I know. It's like, 'Ow, that's not a star, it's a meteorite,' " I said. "That's how we feel."

I thought about that winter when Tommy broke his ankle and had to shelve his magazine idea and I was trying to work. "Maybe the universe is much more conservative than we think," I said. "Like I keep thinking all it wants me to do is what my heart desires and write books and have a bohemian life, but maybe it's really shouting down at me, 'Get a job, you fucking hippie!' "

Isabel laughed. "Except that if that was true, everyone with tons of money would be happy."

"I know," I said, and then said what I actually believe, which is that things usually go wrong when you're still not telling the full truth, or maybe when you're attached to the ways things should be. Like you have to write one kind of thing, or you have to work three jobs to get by instead of one. It's a constant conversation: Is this thing I thought I wanted making me happy? Is it still?

"It's so funny," I said. "When we moved here I thought we would be those people who had it figured out—who were able to keep New York salaries but live a nice life in the country and not have to work endless hours and still have a higher quality of life. But we're still working and striving."

"Yeah, well," Isabel said, "it's interesting that so many of us moved from the city to the country to have these simpler lives and none of us bought small houses."

Across the pale green fields the lake was bright blue.

"It really is nice here, though," Isabel said.

"Yes," I said. "We still have this."

Recipe: Simplify Your Life Quaker Tzatziki

I call this Quaker Tzatziki, because I don't want to offend any people of Greek descent who *really* know how to make tzatziki. (Also Quakers like to live simply.) I like to have a bowl of this available at all times, because if you make something vegetarian like a pot of lentils or couscous and it doesn't turn out well, but you have people coming over for dinner in ten minutes, you can always put this on top of it and it will taste much better.

1 quart plain yogurt (Greek yogurt makes this recipe easier.)

3 to 4 cloves of garlic chopped or 1 tablespoon scape paste (see Scape and Olive Oil Paste, page 166)

1 large cucumber, seeded, peeled, and chopped (I like to put the seeds in a bowl in the fridge and rub them on my face before bed. Cucumber is supposed to be very soothing for the skin, especially after a day in the sun.)

Juice of one lemon

Salt and pepper to taste

A handful or two of fresh dill

1. Put the yogurt in a colander lined with a cloth napkin, and put the colander with yogurt in it into a bigger bowl, so the water can drain out of the yogurt. Let sit in the fridge for a few hours. Pour out the drained water, and transfer the yogurt that's left into a bowl. (Separate it from the cloth napkin, of course.) This will give the yogurt the nice thick consistency of Greek yogurt. Or you could just buy Greek-style yogurt and skip this step.

2. Combine the scape paste or garlic, chopped cucumber, lemon juice, salt (I use about a half a tablespoon to one tablespoon of sea salt), pepper, and dill in a bowl and mix. (You can use a handheld electric mixer for a smoother consistency, but I've found that the cucumber just gets jammed up underneath the blade. One of these days I am really going to have to find my food processor lid.) Let sit for at least half an hour.

3. Mix the yogurt in with the rest of the ingredients and let sit for at least an hour (overnight is best). Salt and pepper again to taste. Serve with fresh bread or on top of any vegetarian dish.

 ——————————————————————————

How to Enjoy Your Work Again

--- ✳

March 25, 2011

Last night in my yogic contemplation class, we had to break our lives down into two areas: career and relationships. We meditated for ten minutes and then described what a good day in one of those areas would look like for us. I chose career.

"Write it in the first person," Amy said, "as if you're already experiencing it."

I wrote,

> *I am approaching my work with excitement and joy.*
>
> *I love what I'm working on, and the hours I'm at my desk pass quickly.*
>
> *At two o'clock when I close my computer, satisfied and happy, I am ready to play with my children instead of screaming at them to give me one more minute while I finish this goddamn email.*
>
> *My work is nourishing, the house is clean and light.*
>
> *My children are thriving with their bright, open, happy hearts.*
>
> *Enough money is coming in to fix up the house and go out to dinner a little more often.*
>
> *I am confident. I am light. I am hopeful and loving.*

"Now," she said, "go home and think about reconfiguring your life, putting that good day first."

I don't even know if that's possible. But if it were, it would be pretty great.

How to Get Your Needs Met, Part 2

✳

April 22, 2011

On Tuesday morning Mom went into the hospital with a possible blood infection. I went to visit her on Wednesday morning. She was lying in bed, pale and fading in and out. "You don't seem quite as bad as you did last time," Dad was saying, referring to an episode she had a few years ago with the same thing.

"I'm not quite as out of it," Mom said, and then closed her eyes.

I looked at them: him in his neat button-down shirt tucked into his Levi's, glasses hanging around his neck and shirt pocket bulging with pens and a magnifying glass. Mom in her dark-blue sweatshirt, my great-grandmother's engagement ring still on her wedding finger. They're getting older, I thought, looking at their sweet, familiar profiles. That's two old, married people talking.

"I need to stop doing so much," Mom said, which is something she says every time she ends up in the hospital for doing too much.

Some nurses came in to take blood and check her stats, so Dad and I went to get lunch.

"What happened?" I said, when we sat down with our trays.

"What do you mean?" he said.

"Why did you bring her to the hospital?"

"It seemed like the same thing as last time," he said, which I think means she probably couldn't stand by herself and had a high fever—my parents are often cryptic about their health. Part of it is not wanting us to worry, and part of it is probably fear. Part of it is probably dignity. Or something. I don't know. Who knows why my parents are the way they are?

"I just think she's overtired," he said. "She was gone from dawn till dusk yesterday."

I looked out the window, that familiar tension between fear of losing my mother and not having enough of her stirring in me.

"She has to slow down," I said.

Dad looked at me. "She likes doing her volunteer work," he said. "It gives her fulfillment."

They're like a fortress, the two of them, I thought. He'll defend her choices to the death, and she'll keep making them because it's her life's work and it *does* give her fulfillment. But maybe also she's afraid of what will happen if she stops.

And I'm afraid of what will happen if she doesn't.

Dad went back to his sandwich and I finished my soup. I remembered when my brother-in-law Peter's mother died. He was in his twenties—too young—and had only been dating my sister a year or so. She was in Africa in the Peace Corps when it happened and he couldn't reach her, so he called Mom to let her know. He didn't know my mother all that well yet, but when she answered the phone he said, "Oh, Barbara. She died." And started to cry.

I teared up a little thinking of this now, because there is something about Mom that makes you tell her what's really in your heart even if you meant to say something else, like "hello," and that's why so many people need her. Including me. And my sisters. And my father, who tenderly ties her shoes for her every morning when the arthritis in her legs makes it too hard for her to bend her knees.

Later, Maria and I rode back from the hospital together. (No real diagnosis—a possible blood infection, but they caught it in time so they should be able to treat it with antibiotics.)

"She should stop driving people to and from jail," Maria said in the car on the way home.

"Or doing all that work at the library," I said. "Dad said she was barely even home yesterday."

"Of course not," Maria said. "Busy, busy, busy."

"I just get so mad when this happens," I said. "I don't mean to be an asshole, but she's always running around helping people and then she gets high blood pressure or septicemia or some other thing that lands her in the hospital and sometimes I wish she would quit helping people and sit in a chair and read books for a while."

"I think she thinks that if she doesn't do it, no one else will," said Maria.

"Maybe it doesn't need to be done," I said.

I sighed. I always feel like such a jerk complaining about Mom. It's like being the one person who doesn't get along with Buddha. Like everyone else is saying, Buddha is so amazing and he changed my life and we're so lucky he's on the planet, and you're the one frowning in the corner saying, "That guy has a weight problem."

"I don't think you're being an asshole," said my sister.

No, I thought. Just acting like a child.

"Thanks," I said. Then, "You're going to be a great mom. I hope someone picks you for their baby soon."

When I was tucking Liam and Dawson into bed that night, Liam said, "Mom, what's the scariest thing in the whole world?"

"The scariest thing to me would be losing people I love," I said. "Like Grandmama, or you and Dawson."

"No," Liam said. "I mean *scary*. Are vampires real?"

"I think it's hippos," Dawson said, and shuddered.

Now it's Friday and Mom is home, driving people who don't have cars to and from jail to see their loved ones as if nothing ever happened.

Meanwhile I turned in my second novel revisions last week. This week my editor left the company.

How to Get What You Want

———————————————————————— ✳

May 7, 2011

Last week Liam and Dawson listened to Johnny Cash's "A Boy Named Sue" nonstop. Liam was a little upset about the part where Sue's father cuts off a piece of his ear ("That part has always bothered me, too," I said), but Dawson loves it.

Yesterday after lunch I was up in the front room reading to Liam while Dawson was in the playroom/bedroom where Tommy was organizing their wardrobe.

"My name is *Sue*!" Dawson was yelling. *"How do you do!"*

"Very well, thank you," said Tommy, who was trying to explain the clothing system he'd set up. "Now see," he continued, "this is your side, and this is Liam's. Your shorts are here, short-sleeved shirts are up here—"

"*My name is Dawson!*" Dawson yelled. *"How do you do! I love you, Daddy!"*

"He never gets the words right," Liam said.

And yet somehow he does, I thought.

Later in the afternoon we all drove out to meet the eight-months-pregnant woman who, just last week, chose Dave and Maria to be the parents of her baby—contingent on meeting them and the rest of us, since extended family seemed to be so much a part of their lives. I rode with Mom, Dad, and Maria, who wanted us to know what we weren't allowed to say to the prospective mother. No last names, she said. Nothing about where we live or what Dave does for a living, no comments about smoking because the mother smoked throughout the pregnancy.

"My friend Charley says the only time his mother put down a cigarette when she was pregnant with him was to pick up a martini," I said. "And he's fine."

"And you," said Maria. "Don't start asking questions about the father of the baby or why she's giving it up. And don't tell her what you do for a living."

"Why can't I talk about what I do for a living?" I said.

"Just sit and listen," she said.

I don't know why she even asked me to come along.

Nine days later: Maria has her baby. She is the most perfect little rosebud of a child I've ever seen. We've managed to throw together a nursery of clothes, car seats, and other miscellaneous baby items from friends and what we found in our attic. Maria is so happy.

"You know," I said to Mom on the phone today, "when she thought having a baby would make her completely happy, she was right. She's completely happy."

"It really does seem like it, doesn't it?" Mom said.

"You have *another* cousin," I said to my boys that night. "This one will live right down the street from you."

"Yay!" said Dawson. "Will her name be Pipperbottom?"

"No, her name is Sophia," I said.

"When are *you* going to have another baby?" Liam said.

"I'm too old," I said. "I'm not having another one."

"You're not too old," said Liam. "You just lay an egg out of your butt."

"Hah hahahahahhahahha," he and Dawson said, at the thought of me laying an egg out of my butt.

"Listen," I said, a little annoyed at being compared to a chicken. "My body makes eggs all the time. I was born with them. Sometimes they grow into babies and sometimes they just get absorbed into my system, but I *can* make eggs and I don't have to lay them."

There was silence.

Uh-oh, I thought. This is one of those times Tommy keeps talking about when I seem to forget that they're children and tell them too much.

Then Dawson burst into applause. "Fan*tas*tic, fan*tas*tic!" he shouted, slowly clapping his hands.

I started laughing. That is exactly the right way to respond to that information. Fantastic! Mommy is even more powerful than we thought! Or something! Either way, I'm not to be taken for granted.

Later that night we had a thunderstorm and in the middle of the night both boys woke up. Dawson was barking like a seal, probably from the croup, which woke up Liam.

"Dawson is terrified," Liam said. "He had a bad dream."

I went into the bathroom with Dawson so Liam could settle down, turned on the light, and sat Dawson on the closed lid of the toilet. "What were you scared of?" I said.

"They're in my head," he said. "I just can't get them out once they're in there."

"What's in there?" I said.

"Scary things," he said. "Monsters. War."

"Those *are* scary things," I said. Then I told him that I used to get scared too, in the middle of the night, and the thing that helped me was just to repeat "Mommy and Daddy are nearby, this is a safe house. This is a safe place," until I believed it.

"What if it's not safe?" Dawson said.

That's what keeps me up at night *now*, I thought, but I said, "You don't have to worry about that."

I knew it wasn't a good answer. How do you reassure your children that they're safe when the world is so frightening sometimes and they know it? I thought of something my mother said once when I was worrying about something—war or disease, probably. "The world is such a dangerous place," she said. "I know it's a hard truth when you have small children. But in the meantime, Becky, *life* is happening."

I looked out the window. The rainstorm was clearing and I could hear a screech owl calling.

"Dawson!" I said. "Come listen."

"Oh!" he said. "It's like a waterfall singing."

I opened the bathroom door. "Liam," I said. "Come in here."

Liam, who was still awake, came happily in and there we stood, up in the middle of the night, listening to the creatures outside, while the clouds drifted away and the moon and the stars shone through. I felt so cozy with them, looking at that soft, blue backyard, listening to the night creatures.

"What a night!" said Liam. "Look at the stars! Look at the white trees!" he said pointing to the cherry trees, blooming hopefully under the moon.

"I know," I said. It's like being awake in a dream.

"Now back to bed," I said.

"Will you sleep with us?" they said.

I sighed and got into bed with them. "This is the last night I'm going to do this."

"Forever?" said Dawson.

"Forever," I said.

"Maybe," said Dawson. "But you'll forget about it sometime and do it again."

How to Save Your Marriage

---- ✳

May 12, 2011

The problem with this whole do-what-you-love-and-the-money-will-come idea is that sometimes it takes awhile for the money to show up.

And in the meantime, you spend a lot of time freaking out about it, which is so stressful! It seems like all Tommy and I talk about lately is money and time. He's been working three jobs this semester—his day job at the college, teaching his adjunct course and making the magazine, and copyediting for *Glamour* three days a month. (Although he does keep coming back from New York with lots of advice.

"You can't wear your bras two days in a row," he said last month. "They need a day of rest."

"Pink lipstick is in!" he said last week. "Short hair is out!")

I have the kids and am waiting to hear back from my editor about the book while writing an article on the history of American whiskey.

Today we went to marriage counseling (we've been going for bi-monthly "tune-ups") and all we did was talk about who was working harder.

"I moved here because I thought this was the only place you could be happy and I could be happy anywhere," Tommy said. "But it's hard for me to be in a place where my industry doesn't mean anything."

"Then we can move," I said. "It's not worth it to stay here if you aren't happy."

"We can't just move," he said. "We can't get financing for another house and you'd miss your family too much."

"I feel like you keep blaming me," I said.

"I'm not blaming you," he said. "I'm working three jobs, I never see you or the kids. When we moved here I banked on your talent as something that could support us, and it's been frustrating to see you not doing anything with it."

My eyes filled. "I am trying to do something," I said, "but I don't have enough time to work. The house needs attention, so do the kids, you're never home, and when you are home you're short-tempered."

"Both of you are professionally wounded," said Teresa. "You're working hard and not making ends meet, and it's very difficult to take care of each other when you're in pain."

"Be tender with each other," she said. "Say *please* and *thank you*. Tell each other things you like about each other."

We sat there, not quite touching, on the couch. I looked at my hands and thought, But what if we've forgotten how?

When we got home I went into my study and Tommy went outside to work on the lawn.

"Mommy!" Dawson said urgently. "I have to tell you something! I left toilet paper in my butt all day! And it didn't even itch!"

"Oh," I said. "That's very interesting."

"Yes it is," Dawson said, heading downstairs for a snack. "Yes. It. Is."

"At least the kids are all right," I said to my mother later when she called to see how things were going.

"Oh, we worried about money all the time when you were little," she said. "Your father had a job that required a lot of travel, and then I got a job and you were sick with tonsillitis a lot. It was a very stressful period of our lives when you were in grade school."

Then she told a story of coming home after an especially hard day of work and sitting at the top of the stairs in the house we grew up in, talking to Dad.

"You and Maria were supposed to be in bed, but you were so dear, you came out and started talking to us too, and then there we were, the whole family in that tiny space at the top of the stairs in the hallway, all sitting there talking. And I thought, This is all that matters. Just this, right here."

Maybe that's what raising kids is, I thought. A series of minisalvations. A string of small moments when even though things are bad, you get glimpses of how we have everything we need right in front of us.

Later after I put the kids to bed I went down to the kitchen where Tommy was doing the dishes. He had a green dish towel with white flowers on it over his shoulder and I looked at his profile, which I've always loved. I made myself some tea and sat down at the kitchen table.

"I'm sorry," I said.

"For what?" said Tommy.

"For everything," I said. "That I'm so slow. That I don't thank you enough for what you do for this family. That I leave my clothes all over the bedroom and hate cleaning up and can't seem to make a meal without throwing food on the floor."

"You really do make a mess." Tommy laughed. He drained the sink and came over and sat down at the table across from me, and we sat there for a minute, listening to the noises of our house—the hum of the refrigerator, tenants moving about in other apartments, laughing or talking and playing music.

"What if we don't make it?" I said. "What if my book is a wash and all of this turns out to be a failed experiment?"

Tommy was quiet. "That would be sad," he said, finally.

I know, I thought. It would be.

"I'm still banking on your talent," he said.

"Really?" I said, a lump rising in my throat. I didn't know how much I needed to hear that.

"Yes," he said. "I just wish it was making a little more money right now."

I laughed. "A-men to that," I said. "You and me both.

"And I'm still banking on your vision for your magazine," I said, as we shut off the lights and went up the stairs.

Then we had sex. So, marriage counseling works.

How to Deal with Rejection, Part 2

    ✳

June 13, 2011

Today my new editor called to talk about my latest revision.

"First of all, I love the main character," she said. "She's funny and warm and I really identify with her."

"Great!" I said, and held my breath, waiting for the "but" I knew was coming.

"But I think we need to revisit some things like stakes for the character and overall structure and also why she keeps making the choices she does. . . ."

"I don't like the book," I said. It came out before I could stop it.

There was a pause on the other end of the line.

"I'm sorry," I said. "I just don't think it has any soul."

There was another pause, and then my editor let out a sigh of relief. "Yes," she said. "I agree."

Neither of us said the words "not publishable," but they hung there, unspoken.

Fuck, I thought. I don't even remember what we said next, just that it ended with her saying, "Why don't you take some time and think about what you might want to do next," she said.

"That sounds good," I said, although "Why don't you go to a bar and put your face in a vat of bourbon?" sounded a lot better.

I went downstairs where Tommy was doing the dishes.

"It's not publishable," I said, sitting down at the kitchen table.

"Did she say that, or did you?" Tommy said.

"We both did," I said.

I went to our pantry, got a bottle of whiskey, and poured myself a shot. "This time I'm not being hard on myself. It's just the truth."

Tommy put his dish towel down and sat across from me.

"I'm sorry," he said.

I drank my shot.

"It's just not where your head is right now," Tommy said.

"I know," I said. I looked out the window at the trees, standing still and peaceful as if nothing ever changed. "I just kept thinking I might be able to save it."

All that time. Those characters I loved so much.

Tommy came over to my side of the table and put his arms around me.

I leaned against him. "What are we going to do?" I said. "We can't give back the advance, we spent all the money."

"It's okay," he said. "We'll figure something out."

"How?" I said, blowing my nose.

"I don't know," he said. "But we will."

How to Quit Everything

--- ✳

Oh, when will it end?

This week Tommy, who had volunteered to take on more responsibility at his day job in the marketing department in return for a raise, was told that yes, he could have more responsibility, but there was no budget for a raise.

"Should I just quit?" he said.

We were in the kitchen when he told me this. He was opening a bottle of wine and I was making a stir-fry with the piles of vegetables that were on the kitchen counter from our farm share.

"If money weren't an issue," I said, "what would your heart tell you to do?"

"I think I'd like to be a stay-at-home dad," he said.

I almost hit him with a zucchini. If that was the case, why on earth were we making this magazine, an ambitious project that takes a lot of work?

"You didn't like being in the house all the time the last time you were a stay-at-home dad," I said.

"That's because we didn't have any money," he said. "And I broke my ankle."

"Okay," I said carefully. "But if I get a job then I can't help you with the magazine."

"I know," he said. "Actually, what I'd like is to have one job, and have it be finishing the magazine."

We are exhausted.

Two days later he got an e-mail saying that there was no funding to continue his course or his magazine through the college next year—which means the issue we're finishing now will be the only one we're funded to do.

Then his boss at *Glamour* called, asking him if he wanted a job working two weeks a month in the city, so Tommy quit his job here.

I feel like we have sunk to the bottom of a pool and are just lying there, waiting for the next tide.

"What are you going to do?" Isabel said yesterday.

"I don't want to make any sudden moves," I said.

Sudden moves based on fear tend to wreak havoc. Sudden moves based on inspiration tend to work out a little better.

"Do you think we should just not finish the magazine?" I said later, when I woke up in the middle of the night and Tommy was awake, too.

We tried a bunch of ambitious projects—but maybe it's just too much work. It's not good for the children to have all of this stress in the house. Not to mention us and our marriage.

"I'm not quitting the magazine," Tommy said. "We've come this far, it's a good product, the students are excited about it, and I want to see it through."

Good answer, I thought.

It will be okay, I told myself as his breath deepened. We'll be fine. We'll figure everything out. If we have to sell the house and move, we can sell the house and move. We still have our health and our children and our friends.

And in my secret heart of hearts, I'll admit I am optimistic. I can't help it. There's a small voice in there saying, You were brave to say you didn't like your book. And Tommy was brave to quit his job in the name of work that's meaningful to him. This is the way. This is the path. You'll see. There is a tiny part of me that's relieved, like breaking up with someone who looked perfect on paper but you knew, deep down, wasn't the one. Maybe this will be good. Maybe it will open up something new.

Right now, however, I think it's time for a good nap.

So, Plan F. Tommy finishes local magazine made by students who have all left town for the summer or graduated. Rebecca never writes again. (But agrees to help him finish the fifty-some pages of editorial that need to be edited and fact-checked.)

How to Soothe an Upset Child

✳

September 13, 2011

It's been a few months, and I have been trying not to be upset about putting the novel down, or the fact that Tommy is traveling again. I have been trying to stay positive, but this past week I've been so depressed. It seems the kids and I fight about everything when Tommy is gone. Yesterday Dawson wouldn't put his pants on. He was so stubborn about it that I ended up leaving him home while I took Liam to school. When I came back, he was sitting on the heater, still not wearing pants.

"Dammit, Dawson!" I said, and started scolding him about taking responsibility for himself, and how I couldn't do everything around here by myself and sometimes you just have to get up and put on your #*&%$! pants whether you like it or not.

"Dammit you!" Dawson said. "I don't like it when you rush me!"

Then he started to cry, and I felt like crying, too.

"I don't want to go to school," Dawson said.

"I know," I said. "But you have to go to school."

"I want to stay home with you," he said.

"Oh, Dawsie," I said. "I'd love to have you stay home with me. But I have to work on my article and you need to learn things."

Dawson looked at his feet. "You always have to work," he said.

I know, I thought. Dammit me.

I sat down next to him. I thought of something my yoga teacher had suggested in one of my meditation workshops, which was that when you find yourself in a difficult situation, ask yourself, "Is there any way I can bring enjoyment into this?"

Dawson leaned against me, and I took a moment to soak in that closeness.

"Okay," I said. "Here's what we'll do. You can come to the coffee shop with me this morning. We'll get a hot chocolate and some breakfast, just you and me, and then we can go to school. But you are going to have to explain to your teacher the reason you're late. And you need to put pants on."

Dawson got dressed and we walked to the coffee shop together. He was so happy on the way down, holding my hand and chatting about where bats came from. (Caves. And sometimes the mouths of great creatures.) I thought, Okay—this was what we needed. Just some time alone together. We had a sweet hour at the coffee shop, and then when we got to school he started getting upset about having to tell his teachers why he was late.

"Can't you do it, Mommy?" he said.

"No," I said, filling out the paperwork for dropping him off late.

"Reason for lateness," the form said.

"Child would not put on pants," I wrote.

"I've had days like that, too," said Stacy, who runs the front desk and who I'm sure has heard every excuse in the book.

Dawson's classroom teacher, however, was a little more stern.

"That's not a good reason to be late for school," she said firmly, but not unkindly. "You've missed the morning sign-in and circle and now we have to get you caught up. I don't want to hear this kind of excuse again."

Dawson looked downcast, which made me want to take him back home with me, even though I knew this was what he needed.

"Go put your coat in your cubby and help us work with numbers,"

Dawson's teacher said, gently putting her hand on his shoulder. Dawson went to his cubby.

I left glad to have him in good hands, but worn out, too. Another morning of struggle, and it wasn't even ten o'clock.

"It's like the second they get up they start saying no," I said to my mother later, when she called to see how I was doing. "And it's like that all day long. Nothing is easy."

"That's probably how they feel, too," she said.

"I know," I said. "That's the worst part."

"You know," Mom said, "I think that all any child wants is a happy mother." Then she went on to say something about the other day, when she was listening to me talk to my father about why I cry in church when people sing—that it's because the world is so full of danger and hardship that when people come together in church and sing about peace it feels like a miracle. "And I just thought," my mother said, "where is the joy in her life?"

I was quiet, thinking, I don't know. I'm trying. I feel completely lost about my work. I don't know what to write. I don't know how not to write. I hate housework, and that's what I spend the majority of my time doing, endlessly moving stacks of things from one place to another. I'm worried that the kids eat too much peanut butter and not enough broccoli.

"I'm fine," I said. "I mean, I *am* happy," I said, although it felt stupid to say it because when someone has just asked you where your joy went, it's pretty hard to say, No, no, I am joyful. Look! I do yoga. I meditate now.

"Your boys are so sweet and they love you," my mother said. "Take them to the movies. Or just loosen up."

Sure, I thought. I'll do that. Easy for her to say. Although I know she's right. Why don't we just have a little fun around here?

Oh, I don't know where my joy went. I just don't know. And I keep hearing myself say bitter things: *That person's an idiot*, or *Those people just don't get it.* A few weeks ago, Tommy and I went to a dinner party, and on the way home I was talking about one of the guests who I felt had spent the whole night telling me how special her hedge fund was because they did pro bono projects.

"Like that isn't worked into their PR budget," I said. "I felt like saying, 'You really want to do something pro bono? Give me fifty thousand dollars and don't tell anyone.' "

Tommy didn't say anything, and in the silence that followed I heard what I'd just said.

"Am I just becoming one of those people who never has anything nice to say about anyone?" I said, and Tommy said, "Not yet, but you have been saying a lot of negative things lately."

I looked out the window. The moon I loved so much was doing her best to shine through a thicket of clouds. This isn't my heart, I thought.

"What happened to me?" I said.

"You're sad," Tommy said. "You've been writing and writing for years and nothing's going out in the world. You're not making money, you're not getting recognition, and that's hard for you."

Why do I need so much? I thought. Why isn't this enough, this house and this life and this family and this man?

Why can't I just be happy?

How to Know What Your Heart Wants

——————————————————————————————————— ✳

September 20, 2011

Last night in yoga we were talking about living in the heart, and the teacher said that we've always known that the mind speaks to the heart, but now science is showing us that the heart speaks to the mind.

That happened to me with Tommy, I thought. I remembered the day I knew I would marry him. I was looking out the window from his friend's apartment and I saw Tommy standing there quietly in his yellow sweater, helping someone move his furniture from one place to another. And it was as if a voice in my heart spoke to my head. "That's your husband." We'd only been out about three times, but it was as if I didn't have a choice, it was already done. My mind could run around in circles and say whatever it wanted, but somewhere I knew that I was going to marry Tommy Dunne and I knew somewhere that he knew he was going to marry me.

I could hear my heart so clearly in those days. Now it seems I have to work harder to listen to it, when it used to talk to me all the time. What does it want now? I think it just wants to help Tommy with the magazine. No, mostly my heart still wants me to make wonderful things. To have a life where I can make a living doing something

I love, and still be connected to family, the earth, and all the life around me.

Is that too much to ask?

"I don't think so," said my yoga teacher.

I love her.

PART FOUR

Crawling Out *of the* Rubble

September 2011–January 2012

How to Transform Your Anxiety into Excitement

✳

September 28, 2011

I have started doing private life-coaching sessions with my yoga teacher Amy about how to find my way back to the soul of my work. (I know. I can't even write it without feeling like a cliché, but what can I say? Desperate times call for people who walk around in stretchy pants, seem very happy, and burn sage.)

"I feel like I lost my way," I said today in our first session.

"Like I can't trust my instincts anymore. You know? And then there's a part of me that *knows* there's something good somewhere in the work I've been doing for the past three or four years. But I just can't see it."

"It sounds like you do trust yourself," Amy said. "You know you have something good, you just want to get back to finding the joy in it." And that, she went on, is not something you can force. "You've tried everything else," she said. "You keep working and working but you can't muscle your way through this. Why don't you just stop?"

"What?" I said.

"Look," she said. "It sounds like you've been someone who has over-functioned most of your life and so far that's worked for you, but now you're about to evolve to a different level, and that's why so many of your old habits are hitting resistance. Take a break, do something you love."

I said I'd been thinking about taking October off anyway. It's my favorite month, and it would be nice to just enjoy it—the weather, the kids, Halloween.

"Great!" she said. "Take a month and only do things that make you happy. What would they be?"

"Maybe Dawson and I will take guitar lessons," I said.

"I'm not sure about lessons," she said. "Think about play."

I came up with a few more things I thought might be play (weed through all the children's clothes and take the ones they've outgrown to the Salvation Army; finish my children's novel; go on a yoga retreat; clean out the house) but were really work.

"No, no, no," she said. "Maybe you need to drink more coffee. Or have some whiskey and go dancing."

That sounded much better.

"You don't have to leave town to find yourself," she said. "You can have an awakening here, with your children and your cats and everything you love."

So. Am giving myself all of October to take time away from my ambition and do what I like. Yoga as much as I want. The coffee shop as much as I want. Writing whatever I'm inspired to write, making clay cats and mermaids. Wouldn't it be nice if this was the way back to making money?

Later, I told my acupuncturist that I am officially taking a break from my ambition. She practically applauded.

"This is so good," she said. "Yes! This feels exactly right."

Then she talked about the menstrual cycle and explained that when you are in the yin cycle—the first fourteen days—you have to slowly build qi back up, and do gentle things, like walking and yoga. This is extremely important, she explained, because this is laying the rich soil for the seed to take root in. Then when you're in the yang phase, you have to be more active and do things like cardio to keep things from stagnating.

"I see a lot of women," she went on, "hugely successful women who are good at their jobs and first in their Ph.D. programs or the head of their company, and they have a terrible time getting pregnant. Often it's because they're brilliant at the yang part of the cycle, but they don't know how to sit still and nourish the soil. So they lose the egg in the second half of their cycle because they didn't allow the yin to make a strong enough place for the egg to take hold."

I said I thought most women in this culture probably weren't good at the yin. Even when we take time off, we're trying to be the perfect mothers or better organizers, or running marathons or packing all the clothes for the family vacation, keeping the car clean, or taking Vietnamese cooking lessons.

Who came up with this idea that we should do everything? And why do we keep doing it?

So now I'm all about the yin. It's like getting a get-out-of-jail-free card. Only exercise vigorously half the month. Have a whiskey cocktail. (But not two, because then I start arguing with my sister.)

Can this possibly be the way to being better at your job?

"Start simply," Amy said. "Ask yourself—will I really enjoy this? Or do I think I *should* enjoy this?"

I went home and made a list of things I enjoy. Yoga (but only if I can walk to the class). Walking. Reading to my children. Cooking. Biking to the farm to pick flowers and raspberries. Dancing. Having tea and reading tarot cards with my friends. Writing in my journal.

What I do not like:

Being in the car.

Working alone.

Other writers who finish their books in less than a year, and sell lots of copies.

Applying for grants.

How to Quit Your Ambition

--- ✳

October 5, 2011

Today in the parking lot of the food co-op, I heard myself say to my children, "If you two don't stop fighting over the Luna bars, I am going to murder you. I am not kidding."

Then I put my organic, pleasantly raised sausage and all-natural mood lifters into the trunk and got into the car.

"You are kidding," Liam said. "You would never do that."

"Do what?" I said.

"Let us die," said Liam.

Oh, I thought. Of course not. That was a horrible thing to say.

"You're right," I said. "I would never, ever, ever murder you. I shouldn't have said that. I'm sorry."

"Or put us on the curb," said Dawson.

They both started giggling.

"I might put you on the curb," I said, instantly forgetting what I'd just learned.

Liam and Dawson started giggling harder.

"We would have to be *sooo* naughty," Liam said.

"We'd have to say the f-word and the h-word and *shut up*," said Dawson. (The h-word is *hate*.)

"And play with matches," said Liam, happily munching on a Luna bar.

"I think it would probably take a little more than that," I said.

Like sitting in your room way past your bedtime yelling, "*Chookabaka la la! Chooka baka la! It is not night now! It is not night!*" at the top of your lungs, after you've already been fed, bathed, and read to, which is what Dawson is doing now. "*Mama, I need you! Doo doo doo! Ma ma ma ma mam am.* Mommy, Mommy, I love you. I love you. *Mom!* Is it a weeknight? Remember a long time ago, you said if it's a weeknight, we can make Liam and my lunches. So let's go do that now."

But I'm going to forgive him because he called me a few days ago from his grandmother's house, where he'd spent the night, to tell me that he was a pretty good guitar player. "Do you want to hear me?" he said. Then he strummed a guitar tunelessly and sang a song that went like this, "Rock out, come on, Mama, let's rock out. Rock out. I love you, you are so good at what you're doing, come on, let's rock out. Yeah, yeah, let's rock out, I love you so much."

Which is exactly what you should sing to your mother to ensure that you don't get put on the curb.

It's also, by the way, very good advice. I haven't rocked out in a very long time.

 ————————————————————————————

Recipe: Awakening Your Creativity

This is a meditation/contemplation technique my yoga teacher gave me. I do it at least twice a week.

Ingredients:

1 person creatively blocked/frustrated/lost or simply curious about what the hell to do next

1 candle

1 notebook

1 writing utensil (or two or three or eight if you want to draw pictures)

A well-lit, clean, comfortable space, preferably one without too much
clutter. (Although a little creative clutter is good for the soul, if you
ask me.)

1. *Create a space.* Find a spot where you can sit quietly. Make it sacred. Turn off all computers and cell phones, put a few of your most cherished things there or make a little altar. (I made mine on my daybed, which Dawson calls the "daydreaming bed," in the corner of the living room between two windows. I put my statue of Ganesh on a table and some dancing rabbits and cats I made, along with some flowers or chocolate or whatever I hope will make Ganesh happy. Then I light a candle and sit down.)

2. *Ask yourself a question.* It can be anything, from "Should I keep working on this stupid thing?" to "Does this situation have anything to tell me?" to "How can I get more enjoyment out of my life?" Personally, I find that it works a lot better and I get clearer answers when I ask the question I really want to know the answer to ("How can I make more money right now?" or "How can I stop being so mad at that asshole?") than questions that I think are more yogic ("What can I do to be more peaceful about this decision?").

3. *Write, uncensored, for ten minutes.* Or draw pictures—whatever. Just take ten minutes to put down the thoughts and images that are swirling around your question.

4. *Engage.* This is the meditation part: Sit quietly and engage with whatever higher power you believe in—the universe, your deepest and truest self, God. Take five or six deep breaths into your abdomen and let your body relax, your mind quiet a little. I like to start out thanking the universe for a few things, like the ability to do this, or all the gifts I've come into this world with, my children, my husband, the trees. Then just focus on the breath. If you want, focus on your question, then let it go. Breathe. Do this for about five to ten minutes.

5. *Write down what comes up.* It can be a word, an image, a feeling, a grocery list, just write it down. Then put it aside for later. Sometimes it takes a few days to see the message, sometimes it's clear right away. Sometimes you just have to sit with the pain of something so you can make room for whatever feeling is behind it.

6. *If you'd like, discuss with a friend.* (This is a great exercise to do with a partner/collaborator.)

7. *Then: Be open to the alchemy of whatever comes next.*

8. *And finally, rock out.* Come on, Mama, what are you waiting for? What have you been doing all this time?

 ———————————————————————

How to Really Irritate a Husband

    ✳

October 13, 2011

This morning at the coffee shop all the men I usually sit with were sitting at our table writing on comment cards. Unlike yesterday, when they'd been talking about gay marriage while thinning out the papers in their wallets because one of them had a backache from sitting on a fat wallet (full of receipts and lists, not money, he was careful to point out) for fifteen hours driving up here from Florida.

"What's going on?" I said to Andy, who sells restaurant equipment.

"It's a revolt," he said. Management had moved the coffee urns from the table where the sugar and milk were to behind the counter where the baristas were. It was an attempt, said Chris, the manager, who is also one of my tenants and plays piano for the school plays, to rearrange the flow of the store.

Jack, who tunes pianos for a living, was furious because now he was going to have to wait in line while people like me got their specialty cappuccinos.

"It doesn't make sense," he said. "I like to come in here and get my drink and sit down. I don't want to wait in line."

"Exactly," said his friend Wylie, who moved here to retire and spends most of his time helping his son renovate the properties he's bought on Main Street.

"It's also insulting," Jack said. "It's like they think we're going to steal coffee."

"That's right," said Wylie. "When I get to the bottom of my mocha and there's nothing left but chocolate, I like to get up and put a little squirt of coffee in there to improve the flavor."

"Aren't you supposed to pay for that?" I said.

"That's the point," he said. "I shouldn't have to."

Mike, a painter, radical, and general rabble-rouser, said he thought everyone should dress up like an Indian and throw coffee into the creek.

"He just wants to dress up like an Indian," said Wylie.

"It's because he's part Indian," said Kevin.

"I think it's because he likes to dress up," I said.

I don't know why I didn't quit my novel sooner. This is a very nice life. I've been spending my time reading, writing in my journal, cooking, making dates with friends, and reading tarot cards with Isabel, working on a series of children's stories.

Every day I pick the kids up after school, and we read or play chess.

This morning I said to Tommy, "You know what all this striving does? It's like all the things that shouldn't be a burden—writing thank-you notes, having people over for dinner, spending time with our children, visiting my parents—have become a burden. And the things that actually *are* more burdensome—taking the car to the shop, making unreasonable deadlines—are where all our energy is going. It's wrongheaded."

"That's true," said my husband, his eyes on his computer screen. He was copyediting some pages for the website he freelances for.

"You don't sound convinced," I said.

My husband looked up at me.

"I just wish *I* could take the time to stop working," he said. "But I can't, because someone has to make some money."

"This is part of what will lead me to make money," I said. "Trust me," I added.

Although a voice in the back of my head kept reminding me of something I used to say when I dated an alcoholic who did whatever he felt like. "Behind every free spirit, there's always someone else cleaning up the mess."

But then I decided not to pay attention to that voice, because not letting your spirit have freedom is also a mess. We have a whole culture saying that it's self-indulgent and irresponsible to think that way, but what's the true cost of that? We're worn out. We don't have time to think about what we're creating. We've forgotten to listen to the voices of the ocean and the wind.

"Maybe *you* don't have to work so hard," I said to Tommy. "Maybe there's an easier way to do the magazine."

"Maybe," he said, and went back to work.

And yet, when you do give up ambition, you begin to see what you have, other than what you don't have. A new, pretty room of your own that you carved out for yourself in a vacated apartment. The knowledge that giving things up is more nourishing than getting more, that the people who matter are sitting right in front of you with a cup of coffee, wondering how you spent your day, minding your business in exchange for your minding theirs.

Or as my little sister said after taking a spiritually cleansing medicinal herb last week—"This is heaven. Right here in our backyard."

Later I told Isabel and John about that conversation with Tommy and how I feel guilty about taking a break, even if in general I'm much lighter and happier.

"*Ack! Ack! Ack!*" screamed my niece Sophia, whom I was babysitting.

"Every time you start feeling like you should be doing something more," said John, "just imagine Einstein trying to come up with the theory of relativity with an infant screaming '*Ack!*' in the background."

That did make me feel better.

How to Write a New Story

--- ✳

October 14, 2011

Had another session with Amy today, who said that part of what we're meant to do here is feel everything. That there's nothing wrong with being sad, because that's just the flip side of loving things. What's painful is deciding that something sucks or you hate it. In other words, it's the stories we tell ourselves about our lives that create the way we live. So we might as well tell ourselves the best stories we can.

I thought about the stories I've been telling myself: I'm slow. I'm a terrible mother. I can't finish anything. Or when I do, my projects still get stuck. (Like when Dawson was three weeks late and still hadn't dropped and my first book hadn't sold, I remember turning to Tommy and saying, "Everything gets stuck in me! Babies! Books! There could be a whole city in there for all we know!")

"Okay," Amy said. "Those stories may have had their purpose at some point, but how well are they serving you now?"

"Not so well. I mean, I seem very attached to them, but it's not like they're helping around the house or anything."

"Go home and write a new story," she said. "Start with, 'I'm on time.' "

• • •

New stories:

I am on time.

I have made good decisions.

I am building happy, healthy relationships with my children, and we can amend things that aren't working.

Taking a break is exactly what I need to be doing.

I'll get back to work when I'm ready, and when I do, the new work will come easily and with more flow.

I am creating something even now—even in my downtime.

None of this has to be hard.

So: effortless, creative success! That's my new mantra, along with high hopes, low expectations, and will someone please shut the front door so we don't heat half of Main Street.

How to Have a Long-Distance Relationship

✱

October 17, 2011

Single mom, week one: On Saturday, before Tommy left for New York again, we had such a nice family day. I went to the coffee shop, where I did a tarot reading for a friend of mine. (I told him to get out of his relationship. "That's too hard," he said. "Let's do it again.")

Liam rode his bike down and popped his head in the coffee shop to tell me he was going to be next door at the used bookstore. When I joined him a few minutes later, he was on the couch at the bookstore reading, and then Dawson rode his bike down and came in and read too, and then Liam borrowed the phone to call Tommy to see if he could come down and bring some money, because I had spent all mine on a coffee. Then Tommy came down and we all went out for a walk. I was so happy, and outside it was dark and brilliant—the sky mostly overcast with some sun poking through, and the flowers and foliage were deep shades of purple, gold, crimson, and orange against it.

Then today Tommy went to New York, and now we all have lice. Dawson brought it home from his classroom. Tonight when we went to the restaurant next door (we'd all been treated), Dawson said to the owner, "Hey, Jonah. I have *lice*!"

"I had that," said Jonah's daughter Evelyn.

"He's just like you down at the coffee shop," Tommy said later when I called him to tell him the news. "We have fleas! We have lice! Who wants to rent one of our lovely apartments?"

"Well," I said, "I've said it before and I'll say it again—if you have nothing to hide, you have no shame."

How to Find Your Way Back to Brightness

　　　　　　　　　　　　　　　　　　　　　　　　　　　　　✳

October 20, 2011

Single mom, day five.

This morning we were all sitting in the front room, which was full of sunlight. I was reading a book, Liam was trying to see what twenty-four times four was, and Dawson was spelling *stop*.

"S. T. O. P," he said. "That's a tricky word, Mommy."

"Mm-hm," I said.

"You haven't had your coffee yet."

"No," I said, closing my book. "You're right, Dawsie. I need to go get some."

"And I need my cigarettes."

"What?" I said.

"Ninety-six!" said Liam.

"Where did you hear about cigarettes?"

"Everyone knows about cigarettes," said Liam.

"I'm going to marry Liam," said Dawson. "Because I don't have a girl."

"How did you find out about cigarettes?" I repeated.

"I'm going to be single," said Liam.

"Dawson," I said for the third time, "who told you about cigarettes?"

"You," Dawson said.

"I haven't had a cigarette since way before you were born," I said. "And then only once in a while, and I didn't fully inhale."

"That's how I saw it," he said. "I saw all the badness coming into your stomach and then looked up through your throat and saw a cigarette."

I looked at my son. Another nice thing about taking a break for a month is that it gives me the space to fully enjoy my children. The other day I was coming back from the coffee shop and as I came up the hill to our house, I saw Liam standing at the end of our driveway. He was standing there in a pair of too-small pajamas—a shirt that came to his midriff and a pair of pants that ended about four inches above his ankles. And when he saw me he burst into a smile, that wide wonderful smile he's had since he was born. And I thought, that's his essence. That bright, shining smile, those open arms. It was like getting a glimpse of his pure spirit: that joy, that exuberance, that way of running he's always had, with his arms out to the side ready to embrace everything—the wind, the day, life.

He's older now, but as he ran into my arms, I thought, Oh child, this brightness! Always, always find your way back to this, no matter what else happens later.

And now, looking at Dawson, sitting on the couch throwing out a poetic line about life in the womb, I had that same feeling: this is Dawson. A child who sees the unseen so effortlessly, who just doesn't care about the line between the real and imagined.

"I love you both so much," I said.

"Can we watch *Avatar*?" said Liam.

"Actually," Dawson said, "I keep seeing them on the ground. That's how I know about cigarettes."

Then it was time for coffee.

Meanwhile, I wrote sixty pages of a children's novel this week. Am getting back on track.

How to Simplify Your Life

─── ✳

November 1, 2011

This weekend Tommy came home after being in New York for weeks on business and we all celebrated by getting into a fight before noon.

I blame pancakes.

I made pancakes for breakfast because it felt like a special occasion to have us all home and together, but the problem with pancakes is that while they seem cozy and delicious—and they are—an hour and a half later the whole family is suffering from a sugar crash and one son is refusing to wear shoes and your husband is saying, "Maybe I should go back to New York," and the other son is sobbing, "You promised me we would go to Target to buy candy!" when the only way you'd make a promise like that is under the influence of Percocet.

Maybe this is just the nature of a homecoming when one person has been away making money and the other person has been home being a single parent. Everyone feels overworked and out of balance and everyone has been holding it together as well as they can, and the second the family unit is back in its place we almost have to have a fight to clear the air and be ourselves again.

Eventually Tommy took the children to mini-golf and I went for a walk with Isabel, where I told her about our morning.

"Pancakes," she said. "There's nothing like them to make an entire family tired, bloated, and irritable."

"Exactly," I said, happy to be understood, and also happy to be on a walk with my friend. It was a cloudy day, but the best thing about living here in the fall is that even on a gray day the scenery is luminous, maybe even more luminous with that steely background, and things like a black bird on a branch of orange sumac in front of a bright green pasture seem like miracles. When we parted ways at the crosswalk near my house after covering the subjects of work, our home lives, and the backwards ways we all try to help the people we love, I was in a much better mood.

I walked into the living room where Dawson was hiding under a couch holding a cloth devil's tail, waiting to jump out and scare me. All of the Halloween decorations were out, and in the corner by the windows where we put the Christmas tree was an eight-foot-tall naked black branch with dark brown leaves that had dried as if they were still blowing in the wind.

"What a wonderful tree!" I said.

"Do you like it?" said Liam.

"Boo!" yelled Dawson without coming out from under the couch.

"I *love* it," I said. "It's fantastic. We should keep it up forever."

"Daddy helped us," Liam said. "We had to go down to the creek but we're not supposed to tell you that because the water is high."

"It needs some color," Tommy said. "Maybe some streamers, or some of your black cat Halloween ornaments."

I looked at him and was so happy he was back. I love Halloween so much, and one of my favorite parts of it is making a Halloween tree. I hadn't even had time to think about it while Tommy was gone and then when he'd come home I'd started yelling at him about how we needed some systems in place and to be more consistent about getting the children to help out, and then I'd gone for a walk, and here he had taken the kids and picked out this magnificent thing, which was better than anything I would have found on my own. I looked at the room, with half of our old costumes strewn across the floor, and at my husband standing in the middle of it all, hanging a plastic skeleton on the tree.

"I'm so glad you're home," I said. "That's what I meant to say this morning when I was yelling about the systems."

"I thought so," he said. "Maybe next time lead with that."

I spent the afternoon with my children carving pumpkins and putting a blue tissue-paper sky and a big, white tissue-paper moon over the living room windows as a backdrop for our new tree.

At five o'clock Isabel and John and their kids came over and we went out trick-or-treating. It was so great. Everyone was out and people had their porches decorated with pumpkins and skeletons and colorful windows.

Liam went as a pirate, and Dawson was going to go as a ghost but at the last minute he put together his own superhero costume—footie pajamas, sneakers, a blue satin cape with a yellow star on the back, a blue wizard's hat with silver stars on it and a blue turtleneck. Tommy safety-pinned a big yellow star on his shirt and wrote "Star Man" on it, and Dawson was so excited he ran everywhere he went so his cape would fly out behind him. Then he went up to every door and said, "Trick or eat!" and then after he got his candy he'd say sincerely, "Thank you, and Haaaaappppy Halloween!" At one point he stopped at a house that had fake cobwebs and orange lights all over the porch and said, "I'm going to tell them this looks beautiful!" which he did. He was just so energetic and excited, like he could barely contain his delight.

At the end of the night, he and I went home together up Main Street. Everyone else was back at the house and Dawson kept running ahead of me like a little imp, his pointy blue hat on his head, his sneakers pounding the pavement. He wove in and out of a group of teenagers, a set of parents with two children in strollers. Then he would stop, look around, make sure I was behind him, and take off again, running in the night, his blue satin cape streaming out behind him. The sky was blue with gray clouds obscuring the moonlight and the streets were lit with streetlights, and as I watched him running to his own rhythm, full of his own light, I wished I could hold on to the image forever.

When we got home, Isabel and John were there. John had built a fire in the fireplace and everyone was warm. Isabel was talking about the haunted house our neighbors made, and the light from the front porch was streaming through the blue tissue-paper sky and white tissue-paper moon. The house felt full and warm and lovely again, and I felt happy, the way I did when we first moved in.

Later, after the children were in bed and everyone was gone, Tommy and I sat by the fire.

"Wouldn't it be nice if you were always home?" I said.

"I'd love that," he said. Outside a small gang of ghouls ran by, laughing.

"Do you think sometimes that we're just choosing to make our lives hard?" I said. "I don't know what it is, it seems like we are struggling with the same things we were struggling with five years ago."

"What we did was leave the place where we could make money," Tommy said.

"But what would have happened if we'd gone back to New York?" I said. "I guess you would be managing editor somewhere."

"And I would be making $150,000 a year."

"And we would be living in a tiny apartment, worrying about money and our children's preschools, wondering if we should move to the country to simplify our lives," I said.

"Exactly," he said.

And this is the problem with living simply. You bring yourselves with you wherever you go.

Tommy put his arm around me, and I pressed into him, feeling the beat of his heart.

"I just want things to be all right," I said.

"What makes you think things aren't all right?" he said.

I thought of a million things. The news. The broken window I noticed on a tenant's back porch the other day. The mouse I heard chewing in the wall the other night that I should probably kill except that I can't bear the thought of it. The fact that the magazine isn't finished yet, and I'm still not sure what to do next. Our private, secret disappointments in what we think we should have done by now but haven't.

I remembered something a friend of mine who counsels adolescent boys with behavioral issues and is going through a rough divorce said to me the other day while we were waiting to pick up our kids at school.

"The trouble is that people expect things to be all right," he said. "And that's just not the way life is. It isn't fair, either."

But I don't know. I think the trouble is that it's all true. Things are not all right, and they are all right at almost any given moment, *at the same time.* And that's where we get into trouble, trying to pick one or the other, instead of living with them both side by side.

So that's my new mantra. It's not okay. And it is okay.

High hopes, low expectations.

"I love Halloween," I said.

"I think this one was our best so far," said my husband.

Outside, my black cat Ryely stood like a sentry on the porch, gazing out at the street with his deep green eyes.

Recipe: Hard-Boiled Jack-O'-Lanterns and Mummy Heads

I first made these two years ago for a Halloween party and they were all eaten by the end of the night. (Although a friend who saw photos of them on my blog said, "Those look like something a crazy person makes.") I, however, think these are brilliant and continue to make them every year. You can present them as either mummy heads or egg-o'-lanterns, and if you want to make them really gruesome, you could try them with pickled eggs.

You'll need a steak knife and cookie cutters. Maybe a hole punch.

Ingredients:

Several hard-boiled eggs

*Dried cranberries or thinly sliced carrots (For eyes, punch holes in the
carrot slices with the hole punch.)*

Here's what you do:

Peel the hard-boiled eggs, and figure out where the white part
is thinnest and closest to the yolk. (I just keep poking the egg
with a knife until I find a place where I quickly hit yellow—good
for aggression.) Carve a face and gently peel away the whites
where you've carved. The yolk acts the way a candle does in a
jack-o'-lantern.

If carving is too hard, or your kids are too small to handle
steak knives, you can use cookie cutters to make shapes, or make
small craters with a much less sharp knife and put dried cranberries (red eyes) or currants in them for eyes and noses.

You can also use other vegetables for hair or hats. I have used
a hot pepper as a hat. It made my egg look very French. (*"Bon-
jour,"* I said, showing it to Dawson. "I'm not eating that," he said.)

Finally, the nice thing about this is that if they start to fall
apart or you made a bigger eye or mouth than you meant to, you
can always turn them into zombies.

When you're finished, rinse the eggs with water or vinegar
diluted with water to remove any fingerprints. Then, as Dawson
would say, "Trick or eat!"

How to Create a Healthy Home Work Environment

———————————————————— ✳

November 20, 2011

Monday Tommy and I spent the afternoon up in the front office working together on the magazine, which is beginning to look like the project Tommy envisioned.

"I'm so cold," said Tommy. "This is what it was like when I was working up here with that broken ankle, freezing."

"I know," I said. "It's terrible. We've got to figure out how to live better."

"We do," he said. "This is a disaster."

"It's a combination of high expectations for our work and low expectations for our living conditions," I said. "I think we have problems."

"And we're *both* like that," Tommy said.

"I know!" I said. "We need to collectively marry someone else who knows how to make a house nice."

But the whole thing made us happy, as if we were both understood somehow. On the wall were a series of pages from the magazine—a story about a guy who's only generated one bag of garbage in the last ten years, an artisanal bread maker, and a whiskey distiller who turned into an activist against natural gas extraction when the water in his last home in Alabama was polluted by fracking waste.

My abandoned novel is in one corner, there's a fax machine on the floor, and all the winter clothes, which we don't know where to put, are in a big plastic tub in the middle of the floor.

The other day Isabel came over to see if I wanted to go for a walk. "I can't," I said. "I have to figure out how to make this story on permacultural farming work."

"What's permaculture?" she said.

"It's hard to explain," I said. "Which is why I can't go on a walk with you."

She wanted to go upstairs and look at the pictures of the magazine, which I made the mistake of letting her do. She took one look at the room and said, "You two are underwater."

"Right?" I said.

Yesterday, we got into an argument about fact-checking, which Tommy thinks we can do ourselves, and I said if we did, we'd be lucky if we finished it by Christmas.

"The problem is that our sense of time is completely different," I said later to Isabel, when we went for the walk I decided to go on anyway. "He always thinks things take much less time than they do."

"Be careful with words like always," said Isabel, who is seeing the same marriage counselor we do.

"And I always think things take more time than they do," I said, ignoring her.

"And then you spend the whole day monitoring the other person instead of doing your work," Isabel agreed. "It's like the time we needed to finish the holiday window, and John decided it was a good time to go to the library and return a whole bunch of books."

"Or when you're in the bus station and they're announcing your bus, and he decides it's a good time to go get a sandwich," I said.

"I do like to have a sandwich for a long bus trip," she said.

"Really!" I said. "Even if it's boarding?"

"Oh, they usually wait," she said.

Anyway, she went on, the point is that when she and John got like that, she found that what worked for her was just to get away from him and do a task she could do well, like rearranging the jewelry display. "I find if I get him out of my line of vision and focus on doing something I'm good at, things get a lot better."

"Good advice," I said.

The other secret, I think, is to combine your talents instead of using them against each other. I think that's what we need to do. I know when Tommy and I work together, we make wonderful things. Our kids, for example. Our wedding.

We just drive each other a little nuts doing it.

Tuesday after we got the kids to school, I went to the coffee shop and asked my friend Alex if she could help us fact-check the magazine. Then I saw another friend and asked him if he could write a piece for us in a week. Miraculously they both said yes, as did my friend Sarah, who was walking down the street and said she'd be happy to make a few phone calls if we needed fact-checking done.

"I hired three people," I said when I came home to Tommy. "As the executive editor, I made an executive decision."

"Fine," he said. But I could tell he was relieved.

So was I. And Friday, after those people slowly helped us finish the magazine, I thought, Why don't you just stick with what you're good at? I am not good at managing Tommy, who is a grown man and perfectly capable of managing himself. But I am good at going down the street to the coffee shop, looking around, and finding the help I need.

How to Manifest Your Dream

December 8, 2011

Things are so up and down around here! Last week we found out that Mom's kidney function numbers have dropped precipitously, and her doctor wants her to go on dialysis.

She is still considering her options and is leaning toward not doing it.

"Why don't you go out to Oregon?" I said to her. "Spend six weeks with Peter and Emily and see if Peter can take care of you?"

"Maybe," she said.

This morning Dawson said something about how he doesn't like it when my father is stern with him, and Liam said, "Boppy knows that Grandmama has kidney failure. He knows she doesn't have many years left to live and he's frustrated. That's why he's stern. He knows she might die and he's doing the best he can."

How do you know that? I thought.

"Who told you all this, Liam?" I said.

"I can read the tones in people's voices, Mom," he said, as if it was the most obvious thing in the world.

Dawson, who was wearing my glasses, said, "I think I need a pair of these."

"Really?" I said. "Can you see better with them on?"

"When I wear glasses, I see what other people see," he said. "But when I don't, I see things people don't see."

"Like what?" I said.

"Oh, the breath of the trees," he said.

"That's an amazing thing to see," I said.

"They're a little mad right now," he said. "Kind of angry."

I don't even know why I pretend to know more than these little people.

"Can we go to Target?" said Dawson.

"Have a carrot," I said.

Meanwhile our magazine is out and it's a hit!

Last night I got a phone message from our friend Harold, whom we haven't seen in a while.

"I got this new magazine in the mail today," he said. "I'm completely blown away by it."

At first I was kind of like, Oh, rub it in, other people are finishing magazines and they're really beautiful. And then he said, "Great job!" and I felt like Dawson with his second birthday—Oh, happy birthday, *me*! I thought. The printer must have sent copies out to our mailing list already.

Then this morning Isabel called me on the way back from yoga class. "Rebecca! Everyone was talking about *Fresh Dirt* in yoga this morning!"

I called Tommy, who was back in New York. "I think it might be a hit," I said. "Everyone is talking about it!"

"Great!" he said. "I just wish I were there."

"Me too," I said. I really wish he were here, too.

We thought we might sell about twenty-five copies and get a few nice notes from friends and then we would move on. It's already sold a few hundred copies, which is way beyond anyone's expectations for newsstand sales.

Last night Dad cried when he was talking to me about it. "What this magazine does," he said, "is give people hope. And people are *starving* for that right now."

Today I did a contemplation on getting rid of bitterness. I sat still and focused on my breath, until I could feel the place in my head where all of my negative energy was. I felt the throbbing, dark cloud of it. There it is, I thought. That's what it's doing. Then I moved down, focusing on the light in my heart until I could breathe into that and send it up to my brain. Then I breathed deeper, into where my spirit lives until I could feel it, deep in my heart area and throat. And it was as if a voice inside of me said, "Oh, hello! You've come back! I've been waiting for you for so long, I'm so happy to see you!"

And then I started to cry. I sat there on the daybed I use as an office, tears pouring down my cheeks.

Later my friend Elvina said that this is what meditation is all about. Getting through the rage and frustration so you can see what's behind it. Concern. Love.

Hope. Grief.

How to Enjoy Your Family Vacation

———————————————————————————— ✳

December 28, 2011

Last week we all went on a family trip to St. John in the Caribbean. It had been a dream of Mom's for years to spend Christmas with her family on a tropical island and she decided this was the year to do it since she doesn't know how many more trips she'll be able to take. (Which is something I can't quite bring myself to think about, so I keep praying for miracles.) So she took a big chunk of her savings and we all packed up and went.

It was a great trip. We swam with the sea turtles. Went on hikes. We sunbathed on the beach. (The water! The water on those islands—blue, deep blue, sometimes green. It's such a gift!) We cooked huge meals together, we ate conch fritters, had piña coladas. We bickered about child care. We watched television. I meditated on the beach and was joined by a pelican, who flew down and sat next to me.

("They love it when people meditate," my friend Rachel said later.

"He was probably sizing you up for dinner," said John.)

Then on the last night we all got into a huge fight that ended with all three of us girls crying and my mother raising her hand and saying, "May I speak, please? May I speak?"

Well. Is there a family in the world that can live together on a tropical island for ten days without fighting? Never mind, because if there is, I don't want to hear about it.

But how this happened went like this:

We all arrived with our own issues. And I just couldn't seem to relax. I wanted to so badly, but it was like the second we got there all of the feelings I thought I'd had under control rose to the surface. I felt so raw and unmoored and even though we were on vacation, there somehow didn't seem to be any downtime, and Tommy and I had no time to talk about the magazine or what we were going to do next.

One day I was on a walk with my little sister down to the beach. We had been talking about jobs and I was saying I feel so frustrated that we keep trying all these ways to make things work, and the one thing we've done this whole time that was actually a success, the magazine, is something that we don't have the money to do again.

"And I'm not even sure what Tommy wants to do," I said.

"Maybe he shouldn't do anything," Emily said. "Right now he's supporting his family, and that's the responsible thing to do and maybe you shouldn't be off starting magazines."

I wasn't sure what to say. Emily is a yogi. She went to a school to get her degree for social work that studied therapy for the soul. Usually she is all about following your heart. Ten years ago it was my sister who convinced me to go to on a weekend retreat where we spent three days learning to focus on our intentions, have breakthroughs, use the laws of attraction to turn our lives around. ("Good-bye," I said to my friend Betsy as I was walking out the door. "I'm off to join my little sister's cult.")

"Look at Dad," she said now. "He is a brilliant photographer. And Mom could have pushed him to focus on that and make that his life, but he felt like he had to be responsible to his kids and that's what he did. And we benefited from that. He was a good father and a good husband."

"He was gone a lot when we were little," I said. "And now he wishes he'd spent more time on his photos," I said.

"Does he?" said my sister.

I shrugged. I had no idea whether or not that was true, but at the moment I really wanted to be right.

"I'm just frustrated," I said. "It's hard to put your energy into something for so long"—and by that, I meant my book—"and have nothing come of it. I don't think a lot of people"—and by that I meant family members—"know what that's like."

"Lots of people know what that's like," she said. "Look at farmers, look at all of the people who have lost their houses. A lot of people are going through what you're going through."

We were at the beach by then, and I stared sullenly at the sea.

"I'm just worried that you're spending so much time focusing on what you don't have, that you're losing your capacity for gratitude and compassion."

I looked at my sister, thinking, if one more yogi says the words compassion or gratitude I am going to throw a coconut at their head. Honestly! You can't have a negative feeling in this family. "I *am* grateful," I said in a very ungrateful tone. "I thank the universe every day for what I have. For my children, my house, my husband, our health."

"Good," said Emily.

"It's just hard to sit with your pain right now," she said a few minutes later. "I feel like if I give in to it, it's never going to stop."

It reminded me of a friend of mine who hates her job. She's exhausting to talk to because every time you say something like, "You know, you could take some time off," she comes up with ways she can't. And if you say, "Why don't you and your husband get some help?" she'll say, "I hate therapy." After a while I stopped talking to her about it, because she seemed so married to her own disappointment.

I could tell from my sister's face that that's what I sounded like now. Trapped. Angry. Resistant.

"I think now would be a good time for a swim," I said.

"I think that's a good idea," she said.

My sister and I made up, sort of, and then on the last night, she asked us to all go around the table and say what our favorite parts of the vacation had been. I said swimming with the sea turtles. Dave said all of the dinners we'd cooked together. Mom said the day we'd all gone to the beach. It had been the one day she'd made it into the ocean and I remembered being on the beach, looking up from the white sand and seeing her and my father floating in the turquoise water, facing each other and smiling. It was as if you could see their younger selves and their older selves all at the same time, an endless loop of appreciation, and a lump rose in my throat. It was moving to see them—and my sister with her two little kids that she was afraid *she'd* never have and my other sister with her adopted baby she worried *she'd* never have, and my aunt Weezie in her blue suit wading out into the water. I can't say exactly why it was moving but it was, as if the moment wanted to say, "At least we're all here. Even if we love each other in clumsy ways and we might lose each other, we're here now and look at these colors! This radiant sun and this blue sea and this white sand." It was a moment when I was otherwise struggling and then the beauty crept through, I guess, and it was luminous and holy.

Peter said his favorite part was a night we'd gone up the coast to go to Miss Lucy's, a restaurant in a tiny town on the other side of the island. Emily said it was a hike we'd taken down to the old Danish sugar plantations.

"I loved that, too," I said, happy to agree with her on something. We'd hiked down a narrow trail filled with twisted roots of banyan trees to a flat place where there used to be a sugar cane mill and a slave settlement. The whole place was beautiful—the remnants of the mill overtaken by trees and moss growing out of it, the trees growing in the middle of what were once buildings. But it felt so haunted. You could feel it the second you went in—a deep sense of sorrow and pain. Liam climbed happily on one of the structures like a monkey, and the sense of darkness for me was so strong I almost wanted to pull him away, as if to say, "No, stay next to me. Let the plants do their job of clearing out what happened here."

I started telling a story about those plantations that a friend of my father's who lived on St. Thomas told me. He'd said that St. John was one of the few Caribbean islands where there'd been a successful slave uprising. The slaves had managed to overpower the Danes by killing most of them and were able to hold the island for six months, until the Danish government enlisted the help of the French, who sent soldiers over to put down the rebellion. The slaves left on the island knew what was coming—they heard the warnings from talking drums on nearby settlements. They knew that they wouldn't be able to withstand an attack from the French, so they agreed to commit mass suicide. The whole community, fathers, mothers with babies in their arms, and children, held hands and jumped off a cliff into the sea.

There was a "why did you have to tell that story?" moment of silence before my little sister said, "All right, that's *it*. I was just trying to end this trip on a positive note and *that's* what you bring up?"

"I thought it was a moving story," I said.

"I feel traumatized by that story," my little sister said. "I feel sick to my stomach."

Then she said that maybe it was that she was just so tired of having this baby on her all the time, but she was just sick of the way I was refusing to hear anything good, and I said I was sick of everyone telling me to be happier when I haven't seen my husband in three weeks and still haven't had a chance to talk to him because he's the only one authorized to drive the rental minivan and has been driving everyone everywhere. And maybe I was bitter, but everyone telling me to be positive and happy was just making it worse. Maria said why did everything have to be about me? She was bitter, too, when she couldn't have a baby, but she didn't run around telling everyone about it.

Soon we were all shouting and crying and Peter left the room and the other husbands were looking at their plates. I could practically hear Tommy thinking, "Why can't these people just talk about sports and the weather?"

"May I speak?" said my mother finally, raising her hand. "May I please speak?"

There was a pause.

"I think," my mother said, "what no one is saying is that Becky is a little depressed. And when you're feeling like that you don't hear the good things, that's just how the brain works. And we all keep trying to fix her because it's hard to see her in pain, but none of us are acknowledging that she and Tommy have had a tough year and none of us knows what it's like for them right now."

It was as if she opened the door to the grief that was beneath all the anger and disappointment, and something inside me broke.

"I feel like I *failed*," I said. "I knew it would be hard for Tommy to find work in Ithaca, I knew that. I always assumed that I would be able to help support us with mine. But I couldn't. And I worked so hard on something I didn't like for years, and I was sad, and the kids missed me, and I have nothing to show for it. And now Tommy has to work all the time to make up for it, and it's all my fault and I'm so sorry."

I started sobbing. Everyone was quiet.

"And the one thing we did well," I said, looking at my husband, "is something we can't continue unless we do it ourselves."

Tommy put his arm around the back of my chair, holding space for me, the way he does.

My father cleared his throat.

"I think what no one is acknowledging is that these are hard times," he said. "People are pretending the economy isn't bad, but it is. I look at all of you trying to make ends meet and blaming yourselves, and you know, your mother and I never had to worry about both of us working. We didn't have to think about paying for our own health insurance. You're all doing wonderful, interesting things and taking risks. When I saw the idea for your magazine, Tommy, I wasn't sure if it would work. But when I read it, I thought, This magazine gives people hope. And we don't have a lot of that right now. I'm proud of you. I'm proud of all of you."

Then my Aunt Weezie spoke up.

"Listen. You girls are all upset because your mother is sick. We all are. I'm upset too." She picked up a fork and then put it neatly down by her plate and looked around the table at all of us.

"But I've been a sister and had a sister longer than any of you, and I want you to know that even though those relationships are hard—very hard—" she looked at my mother, who held her gaze, "and sometimes you think they're too hard and you're just going to walk away, they're the most important ones in your lives and maybe the world. And you need to work it out, because your mother *is* sick and you are going to need each other."

At which point those who hadn't been crying started crying, and those who had been crying teared up again.

Finally, Tommy and Dave got up and started to clear the table. I went over to start washing dishes.

My little sister, Emily, put her hands on Maria's shoulders and mine and said, "You two. Tell each other two things you like about each other."

"No," we said.

But eventually, I admitted that I admired the fact that Maria seemed to find being a mother so easy, that she was so respectful of her daughter and never spoke sharply to her and was still able to get Sophia to listen. And Maria said she admired the way I was able to make friends easily and that she liked my bathing suit.

"Troublemaker," I said to my little sister as we passed each other on the way to our rooms.

"You can't stay mad at me forever," she said, putting her arm around me.

"I know," I said. "But I can for a week."

Later, I was thinking that it's so easy for us to think our family members don't like us. And sometimes, of course, they don't like what we're doing or they're sick of our shit. But oftentimes it's just a feeling of helplessness at watching each other suffer. Which means what it really is, is love—even if it comes in the form of your sister screaming at you. I always think of that quote in Corinthians that never quite sat right with me—love is patient and kind, it's never angry or jealous. I've always thought it sells love a little short. Love has so many faces. It's patient, kind, yes, but it's wily, beautiful, fierce, and earth-shattering. Why do we try to make it quiet and small, when it's probably the most powerful force in the world?

The next morning we packed up all our things—bathing suits, tunics, cheerful, brightly colored hats and shorts we would no longer wear when we got home. I went down to the kitchen and sat with my mother. She was wearing a white shirt open at the throat and blue sweatpants and was leaning on the brass-topped cane that Aunt Weezie bought for her. She looked resplendent sitting there in her green hat, radiating calm, her gently lined face relaxed and tan, her blue eyes kind and full of light.

I put my head on her shoulder.

"Thank you, Mom," I said. "I felt so supported by you last night."

"Oh, Becky," she said, hugging me. "You're welcome. Things will get better for you and Tommy. They will. You just keep doing what you're doing."

"I know they will," I said into her shoulder, breathing in her smell. "But then you'll die, and I'll never be happy again."

My mother put her hand on my cheek.

"Everyone dies," she said.

"I know," I said.

I know.

How to Turn Your Bitterness into Something Sweet

January 5, 2012

On New Year's Day, my husband and I had a business lunch to talk about the future of the magazine. He has two weeks before he's due back in New York and we're trying to figure out our lives.

We went to one of our favorite restaurants and sat down. "Okay," I said. "You and I are going to have a conversation about where we are. Not where we think we should be, not where we could be if x, y, and z hadn't happened. But what we have, what we've finished, and how we can move forward."

We made a list of what we have:

A local magazine that came in under budget and sold way more copies than we'd hoped.

A children's book I'd written, and a pile of finished essays I could try to turn into something.

Two healthy children.

A community we loved.

A house with rental income.

For Tommy: A monthly freelance gig with a website, and his two-week-a-month job at *Glamour*, which we could (mostly) live on.

Each other.

"And an Etsy shop," I said. (Tommy didn't say anything: the cats and mermaids still drive him crazy.)

It didn't look bad.

"Okay," I said. "What do you really want to do? If we reconfigure things by putting the life we'd like to live first—not the money, not the house, not the achievement—what would you do?"

"I would do another issue of our magazine," Tommy said. "And also try to make it a national."

I took a deep breath. "Okay," I said. "Let's do it."

"Really?" Tommy said.

"Yes," I said. "I'll help you." This time, we'll do it together.

We decided Tommy was going to work a few more months in the city, while revisiting his business plan to see if we could put another issue of *Fresh Dirt* together without having to go into debt to do it. And in the meantime, we needed to take a break, and clear out the old things from our house to make way for the new.

On the way home I started talking about a new book idea I had, one that took all the essays I'd been writing about us trying to raise our children and carve out a life for ourselves here over the last few years.

"I don't know," he said. "That sounds like it would be a lot of complaining about you not liking to clean the house."

"That will definitely be part of it," I said.

"Do you think people want to hear more about parenting?" he said.

"But it wouldn't just be about parenting," I said. "It would be about life and family and trying to follow your path even when it looks different than you thought it would."

"Hmmm," he said. "That's what your last book was about."

"True," I said, "only that was about drunk people. This one is about small people who act a lot like drunks. 'Ha, ha, I took your keys!' 'I need juice!' 'I love you so much!' 'Oh, please, *please* don't make me wear socks.' "

Tommy laughed.

I thought of when we first came here, how all we thought we wanted was a simple, beautiful life, but what we ended up with was a rich, messy life—a much more expansive kind of beauty. And so many of the things I was afraid of happening happened. Tommy's course was defunded, I gave up on my book. I fought with my husband, yelled at my kids, didn't get enough sleep, let the backyard go wild and the gutter on the front porch leak. My mom got sick, I got depressed. And here we are. I still feel like we're on the right path. It's not easier, or even necessarily happier. But it feels more powerful in a true way— like there's less noise getting in the way of my soul.

But maybe that's just what happens. I always thought finding a life you love would make things easier, but the truth probably goes something more like, Yes, follow your dreams! But they will kick your ass. Although your ass will probably get kicked anyway, so you might as well have it done in the name of something you love.

"It's about finding a creative life," I said. "And trying to raise a family and be connected to nature and good food and friends and all of the things that matter to us and how crazy hard that is, but also how nourishing and sweet it is at the same time."

"Hmmm," said Tommy. "I like it."

"And it would have recipes," I said.

A few days later some friends of ours who worked on the first issue of *Fresh Dirt* called and said they would work for whatever we could pay on a second issue of the magazine in the hopes that it could become a permanent job if we found funding. We're having our first meeting next Wednesday.

Today I'm meeting with my yoga therapist/life coach to see if she has any thoughts on how to approach my new book with as much enjoyment as possible. She'll probably say something like, "Stand on your head!" "Drink espresso!" "Write the whole book at the coffee shop, where you don't have to feel alone!"

To which I say, "Amen!" Less loneliness! More espresso! More time with your feet in the air and your head on the ground.

Epilogue

How to (Finally) Get Your Children to Go to Bed

———————————————————————————————— ✳

Mother's Day, 2012

This Mother's Day we went to dinner at my sister Maria's house. Liam entertained Sophie by letting her jump up and down on his stomach, and Maria, who was cranky because she hadn't gotten enough sleep, said that she felt like she always looked like she'd been run over by a truck.

"How does anyone do it with kids this small?" she said.

"Just buy a nice housedress, cover the mirror with Vaseline, and don't look in it until she's five," I said. "You'll be much happier."

Sophia ran by with a saggy diaper. "Poop!" she yelled. "Poop!"

"Dave," Maria said. "It's your turn to change her."

"I'm making a sandwich," Dave said.

My sister looked like she was about to explode.

"Also," I said, picking up Sophia, "don't worry about your marriage being good right now. You have a long time to be married. If you try to have a perfect marriage on top of the sleep deprivation and diapers, you'll need Ritalin."

We sat down around Maria's table. Mom had just had a series of tests done on her kidneys, and so far her numbers were holding, keeping dialysis at bay. Tommy was home, having just gotten *Glamour* to agree to let him work from home. We'd just had our third editorial meeting for the second issue of *Fresh Dirt* and were excited about the content. (A DIY page. A fashion shoot at our local music festival. A features section on people who are living the change they want to see in the world.) And I had gotten a green light for the book I'd discussed with Tommy—the one I'd been writing the whole time I thought I was supposed to be writing something else.

Dawson ran by the window outside chasing someone (a neighbor child? the dog?) with an uprooted burdock plant. Liam went upstairs to take a bath in Maria's tub and came down wearing a towel.

"Sophie's jumping up and down on your bed naked," he said.

"How did she get out?" Maria said. "Dammit! She's supposed to be asleep."

"She says a lot of dammits," Liam said to me. "She must have to pay Dave a lot of money."

Last night Liam and Dawson asked me to tell them a story about when I was little. I told them about how when I was a girl I used to wake up in the middle of the night scared to death. I would lie there thinking about monsters and ghosts and burglars and all the horrible things that could come into the house and how I would be the only one awake and would have to save myself and everyone else, and then I would be up and terrified and couldn't get back to sleep.

"I know what that's like," said Dawson.

"What did you do?" said Liam.

"I would start to cry," I said. "Quietly at first so no one would hear me, but then I would realize that I *wanted* someone to hear me, so I'd start crying louder. And louder. And then . . . *stomp! stomp! stomp!* up the stairs, and then a huge shadow would appear in the doorway and there would be Boppy, in his blue pajamas with his hair sticking out like a yeti and his beard all crazy and his eyebrows pushed together, and he would say, 'What are you crying about?' And I'd say, 'I don't know!' and start crying louder."

Liam and Dawson began giggling.

"That's like you!" Dawson said.

"I know," I said.

"Without the beard," said Dawson.

"Anyway," I said. "So I would cry and then he'd say, 'Go. To. Sleep.' And then he would go back downstairs, and I would lie awake sniffling, feeling like the loneliest girl in the world."

Liam and Dawson were now shrieking with laughter.

Tommy poked his head in from the hallway.

"Lights out," he said.

"Okay," I said. "I'm almost done."

Tommy left the room.

"Did you fall back to sleep?" Dawson whispered.

"Of course not," I whispered back. "I would keep crying and crying until finally I'd hear Grandmama and Boppy's bedroom door open and then I'd hear soft feet padding gently up the stairs . . . *pad, pad, pad.* And then a shadow would appear in the doorway, a smaller one this time, and it would be Grandmama. She was in nursing school then, so she was very tired. But she'd just pull back the covers and quietly, quietly she'd get into my bed. Then she'd just put her arms around me, and she was so big and soft, I'd stop crying. And I'd snuggle in until I could feel the beat of her heart." I stopped talking then, thinking about my mother and how much I love her. It might be true that what all children want is a happy mother, but a loving mother, even if she's tired, is pretty good, too.

"Keep telling the story!" said Dawson.

"And that's when I'd fall asleep," I said.

"I'd like that," said Dawson.

"Why can't you get into bed with us anymore?" Liam said.

I looked at both of them—Liam's wide blue eyes, Dawson's brush cut, which makes him look like a hedgehog. They're boys now, I thought. Not my little babies. How much longer will I have this sweetness? I picked up the covers and got into bed, snuggling in between them.

"I can," I said.

They tossed and turned a few times, arranging themselves so they could get to sleep, and then they quieted down. I lay there, smelling their hair, feeling their heartbeats, so grateful for their little bodies, their dearness, their eyes and ears, and the way they see the world. All that time, I thought. All that time I spent thinking these little boys were getting in the way of my work, when all that time they were showing me the way. And I kept saying, "Stop! Get out of here, I'm busy." And they'd say, "Okay, we just want to love you all the time," and I'd say, "Go!" and they'd say okay and then they'd run back in and say, "Mommy, look at this! Mommy, can I set this cracker on fire? Mommy, can a duck and a bear get married?" And I'd say, "Please! I just need to finish this," and then I'd turn to my computer and my statue of Ganesh and pray for a miracle.

And here it is. This. This love that was all around me all the time, that is always there, like a light in the dark, waiting to be seen, waiting for us to come home.

Tommy poked his head in the door again.

"Happy Mother's Day," he said.

"Thank you," I said. "I *am* a happy mother."

I extricated myself from the children. "At least for now," I said.

Tommy laughed. "Don't worry," he said. "I won't get used to it."

Later I lay next to my husband, my back against his chest. The light from the moon spilled into our bedroom across the bed. I listened to my children snoring, the spring peepers outside calling to each other across the creek, the squirrels settling down upstairs beneath our leaky roof, our new tenant, Bri, practicing her banjo and singing softly to herself in the apartment next door. I imagined my parents, both still alive, falling asleep together across the lake in the house I grew up in, my sister down the road putting her new baby to bed, my other sister with her two daughters having dinner with her small family in another city across the country. I thought of the trees outside (still here!) and the ocean (still blue in spite of everything we do to it!) moving with the winds and the tides beneath the stars.

Thank you, I thought.

Whoever or whatever you are.

Thank you.

This, I thought, is heaven.

Acknowledgments

——————————————————————————————— ✳

This book would not have been possible without the love and support of my family. I am so grateful for their patience, strength, openness, humor, and light, and for their willingness to be on the page. Thank you, Dad, for teaching me through your own passion for photography and steam engines that loving your subject matters. Thank you, Mom, for still laughing at the Sunday comics every week, for being who you are, and for teaching me to find wonder in both the darkness and the light in the human heart. My sisters are the best. Thank you for being such great teachers—and, for when I say things like, "Well, then, I guess we just can't talk to each other anymore," for laughing as if that is the funniest thing you've ever heard and saying, "You know that's just not going to happen." Thank you, too, for being such awesome women, and for bringing such tender and awesome men, Peter and Dave, into our family. Aunt Weezie, thank you for inspiring me on so many levels. If there were ever a pure creative spirit, it is you.

Of course, I thank my children, who have opened and deepened and lit up my life like starshine.

And my husband. I would be lost without you, Tommy. Thank you for choosing to spend this much of your life with me.

I also deeply thank the people who believed in and helped me with the novel I couldn't finish: Amanda Murray, Jin Auh, Helen Rogan, and Erin McGraw. I wish I could have made that book the book we all hoped it would be, and I hope someday I will. I am grateful for all of your patient, wise counsel with it, and Jin, especially, for saying that you still believed in it even after I had to put it down. I'm storing that in my heart.

This book also wouldn't have been possible without the vibrant community that surrounds us here in this small part of the world where we live. My morning meetings with friends from the coffee shop—Tom, Charlie, Jim, Barry, Greg, John, Vince, and Dan—helped keep me grounded and made writing a delight again. The women at the Lakshmi Institute, who also became my team of midwives that helped birth the book: Amy Abelson, Rachel Bush, Denise Hatch, Kelly Caraher, and Jaclyn Loberg—thank you, lovely goddesses. You've changed my life and made me a happier creative being. Sabrina Weill, Sadie Van Gelder, and Erica Beeney, three brilliant editor/writers and dear friends, thank you for reading and talking and reading and talking more, and making the book better. I feel so lucky to have been able to work with you on all the different levels we've worked together. Elvina Scott, thank you for your old soul and good humor and spectacular listening skills. Thank you, Jane George and Denise Milito, for reading the manuscript thoughtfully and lovingly when it was close to being done. Your support and clear vision really helped move me (and it) forward. I owe you drinks and food.

Many, many close friends walked in and out of my life and home while I was working on this, providing wisdom and depth to everything. Bryan and Anna Root, Katherine Ludwig, Mike Naylor, Emily Rothenbucher, Emily Thompson, Bri Richardson, Hitch Lyman, and Pam Capista are just a few. Domenica Brockman and Justin Hjortshoj, thank you for being such smart, hilarious, and simpatico companions during those years when the kids were small and we were all growing and changing, and for the many hours spent in your kitchen or screened porch or living room, cooking and eating, and for reminding me always, always, of the importance of laughter—especially in the middle of a cold winter. Hillary and Ben Guthrie provided a beautiful, open, light and clear writing space where I was able to finish the manuscript and bring the book to life. Thank you for being such guardian angels.

I also need to thank Rebecca Friedman for seeing the light in these pages before I did and then for tireless work and reading as the book grew and changed. And Molly Lindley, a brilliant editor who read the book again and again, whose wisdom helped me grow the book from a bunch of random pages to something that had a narrative arc. To the people at Simon & Schuster, for letting me find my way with my work and for supporting me while I did. Emily Graff, thank you so much for your help and guidance through the final changes that make a book fully breathe. Wendy Sheanin, thank you for your intelligence, insight, and for fully seeing and supporting what it is I'm trying to do (again!).

And to the spirits of land and the water and the ancestors, who keep moving me forward, thank you. I see you. Thank you for calling me home.

About the Author

——————————————————————— ✳

Rebecca Barry is a freelance writer, author, and writing coach. Her nonfiction has appeared in *The New York Times*, *The New York Times Magazine*, *Real Simple*, *Hallmark*, *More*, *Food and Wine*, *The Washington Post Magazine*, *Best American Travel Writing*, and *Saveur*, among other places. Her fiction has been in *Ploughshares*, *Mid-American Review*, *One Story*, *Tin House*, and *Ecotone*. It has also appeared in *Best New American Voices* and has been short-listed numerous times in *Best American Short Stories*.

Her first book, *Later, at the Bar*, was a *New York Times* Notable Book and a *New York Times* Editors' Choice and was short-listed for the Story Prize in 2007. She is also the executive editor of *Fresh Dirt Ithaca*, a local green-living magazine she cofounded with her husband, and has an Etsy shop full of mermaids and cat ornaments she makes when she's not writing or editing.